Top 110 Authors Of India
World Record Anthology

Readice Publication

Copyright © 2024 by Readice Publication
All rights reserved.

No part of this publication may be reproduced, distributed, or transmitted in any form or by any means, including photocopying, recording, or other electronic or mechanical methods, without the prior written permission of the publisher, except in the case of brief quotations embodied in critical reviews and certain other non-commercial uses permitted by copyright law.

Editor-in-Chief: Tejasvi Vashishtha
Publisher: Readice Publication

This anthology is a collaborative collection featuring original work by individual authors. Each author retains the copyright of their respective contributions. The publisher assumes no responsibility or liability for any errors, omissions, or claims made by the contributors.

First Edition: October 2024

Table Of Contents

1. Monisha Nagendran
2. Aamir Reyaz Shieikh
3. Er. S.Dwarakeesh
4. Akanksha Shukla
5. Nakul Rathi
6. આયુષ અંધારીકર
7. Harsh M. Joshi
8. Muskaan
9. Ishita Verma
10. Bhuvi Gajja
11. Ms Nikhlesh Jaikishan Sejwar
12. Pranav Sheth
13. Achyut Umarji
14. Anjali Jain
15. Delisha
16. Shria Chirvi
17. Santhoshi Choradia
18. Rakesh Kumar Singh
19. Akira Sravani
20. उमेश कुमारी "प्रेरणा"
21. Dr. Sree Varshini R
22. Archita Mohanty
23. Selva Mahalakshmi S (Agni)
24. Asgar Hussain
25. Manju Preetham Kuntamukkala
26. ROHIT RATAN KHAIRNAR
27. DEEPAK BARAI
28. TARIQ AZAM KASHMIRI
29. Suresh Kannan Nadar
30. Prerana Gavhande
31. AKASH MONDAL
32. Archana
33. Pragya
34. Sukriti Yadav
35. AK Dhiman 'Veer'

36. Ramya N
37. UTKARSHAA SINGH
38. Shaikh Shahajad Ahmad
39. Suraj Pandit
40. Manav Chopra
41. Nitika Khanna
42. Sayantani Roy
43. Mehak Amir
44. SAKTHI
45. Anu Rajpoot
46. Soumya Kashyap
47. Aniruddh Sharma
48. Disha Darshan Shah
49. Disha Shah
50. Jeetal shah
51. Vivek Saswat
52. Zainab Mustafa
53. Janvi Pippal
54. सीमीं नईम सिद्दीक़ी
55. Radha Kumari
56. Abismita Das
57. Runa
58. Kiran Rathod
59. Rudra
60. Sangeeta Jolly
61. Ankit Kumar Singh
62. **Sakshi Singh**
63. Dinesh Poswal
64. Aadithyaa
65. Surender Singh Rathore
66. Abhishek Yadav
67. Gulam subhani
68. Aaradhana Aiyyar
69. Aditi Bodhankar
70. Drishti Engineer
71. Anmol Agarwal
72. Kirti Gupta

73. Shubham Singhal
74. Mikhail Xavier Fernandes
75. Pratyasha Bairiganjan
76. Ayush Kumar
77. Sheehan Chakraborty
78. Ajulal C R
79. Aastha Sangwan
80. CHINMAY KHARE
81. Juhi Pathak
82. Akriti Khetan
83. Saloni Tamta
84. Insha Ahmed
85. Nidhi Jaiswal
86. Ananya Khemani
87. Madhusudan S
88. Akshay Sharma
89. Sukriti Kumari
90. Adarshika
91. Snigdha Sarkar
92. Riddhi Agarwalla
93. Swetanshu Singh
94. Ishika Bhatia
95. Durga Yadav
96. Satyam Singh
97. Arindam Mallick
98. Sohamm Joshi
99. Rudranshu Katyayan
100. Saloni Motwani
101. Aayushi Nehra
102. SUJAY D
103. Saptarshi Shukla
104. SAI KARUN NANDIPATI
105. Ishaan Malhotra
106. Asha Verma
107. Priya Nair
108. Amar Singh
109. Meera Desai
110. Raghav Sharma

1. Monisha Nagendran

BEING A GIRL

It's my town, but I'm never free
To walk alone without eyes on me.
Safety has vanished, a bitter decay—
The trust of every woman stolen away.

They tell me to cover from neck to toe,
To avoid becoming prey wherever I go.
They roam without shame, bold and free,
While I'm left in fear, too scared to name

In the shadows, I whisper a quiet plea,
For a world where my spirit can roam free,
Where fear and judgment are left behind,
And I reclaim my peace of mind.

I write the poetry that I cannot live,
Like a free bird with no wings to give.
I love being fantasy in my own galaxy,
Where the world is full of
Positivity and serenity.

Waves of peace erase
All my bruises and scars,
And I live the life I've ached for.
-Monisha Nagendran

2. Aamir Reyaz Shieikh

Whispers of Tranquility

Silence felt in its core, peace flits the heaven,
A faint murmur at the nights serene end.
The quiet flow of rivers and the stars that glitter the night sky bear testament to the graciousness of nature.
Aiding fallen angels gleefully showcasing Gods grace.
Beneath the sky, devoid of any kind of moving substance, so calm and wide.
All of the human problems dissolve, and all of the fears disappear.
Mountains that stand tall with determination as their shield, Watchers of the serene white light.
No war, no tear drop, no bitter sobs,
Just breezes that whistle and songs of mothers.
Through peace, we find the soul's rebirth,
A love so infinite and celestial that it goes beyond the sky and heals the earth.
Let hearts be the unite, and let the hands be laced, Because peace is going to bud as a divine present.

3. Er. S.Dwarakeesh

பொது நுண்ணறிவு (Artificial General Intelligence - AGI):

பொது நுண்ணறிவு (AGI) என்பது மனிதனின் சிந்தனையை ஒத்த, பரந்த அளவிலான அறிதல் திறன்களை கொண்ட நுண்ணறிவு அமைப்புகளை உருவாக்கும் துறையாகும். இந்தக் கண்டுபிடிப்பு மனிதர்களைப் போல சிந்திக்கவும், பிரச்சினைகளை தீர்க்கவும், தன்னிச்சையாக கற்றுக்கொள்ளவும் உதவுகிறது. அதாவது, AGI அமைப்புகள் பலதரப்பட்ட வேலைகளையும், கேள்விகளையும் நுண்ணறிவுடன் கவனித்து செயற்படுத்தும் திறன் கொண்டதாக இருக்கும்.

AGI முக்கியத்துவம்:

1. பயன்பாட்டு துறைகள்: பொது நுண்ணறிவு மனித சமுதாயத்தில் தொழில்நுட்பம், மருத்துவம், கல்வி, தொழில்முறை துறைகள் போன்ற பல்வேறு இடங்களில் பயனுள்ளதாக இருக்க முடியும். இது வெறும் கணக்கீட்டு திறனை மட்டுமல்லாமல், அறிவுசார் முடிவுகளை எடுக்கும் திறனையும் கற்றுக்கொடுக்கிறது.

2. தன்னிச்சையான கற்றல்: AGI அமைப்புகள் விரிவான தரவுகளை பயன்படுத்தி தன்னிச்சையாக கற்றுக்கொண்டு, புதிதாக வரும் சவால்களை சமாளிக்கும் ஆற்றல் பெற்றிருக்கும்.

3. மனிதனை ஒத்த சிந்தனை: AGI அமைப்புகள் மனித சிந்தனையை முழுமையாக பிரதிபலிக்கும் திறன் பெறுவதால், இது பல பிரச்சினைகளை தீர்க்கவும், புதிய கண்டுபிடிப்புகளை உருவாக்கவும் பயன்படும்.

4. மருத்துவ முன்னேற்றங்கள்: AGI மூலம் மருத்துவ சிகிச்சைகளில் முக்கியமான தீர்வுகளை விரைவாக கண்டறிந்து, நோய்களை பரிந்துரை செய்யும் மற்றும் துல்லியமான சிகிச்சை முறைகளை உருவாக்கவும் உதவும்.

AGI எதிர்காலம்:

பொது நுண்ணறிவின் வளர்ச்சியால் தொழில்நுட்ப உலகில் ஒரு பெரிய புரட்சியே ஏற்பட இருக்கிறது. பல தொழில்நுட்ப நிறுவனங்கள் AGI-யை ஆராய்ந்து புதிய முனைப்புகளை தொடங்கி வருகின்றன. இது பலமுறை மனித வாழ்க்கையை மேம்படுத்தும் வகையில் தொழில்நுட்பத்தை பயன்படுத்தவும், புதிய கண்டுபிடிப்புகளை மேற்கொள்ளவும் உதவுகிறது.

AGI மனித சமூகத்தில் மிகப்பெரிய தாக்கத்தை ஏற்படுத்தும் ஒரு மிகப்பெரிய துறையாகவே விளங்கும். இதன் மூலம் அனைத்து துறைகளும் நவீன தொழில்நுட்ப மாற்றங்களுக்குத் தகுந்த வகையில் மாறும்.

தொடர்புகள்: துறையில் மேலும் ஆராய்ச்சிகள் நடைபெற்று, உலகளாவிய மாற்றங்களை உருவாக்குவதற்காக, AGI ஆராய்ச்சி மற்றும் பயன்பாட்டில் அனைத்து மக்களும் ஆர்வம் கொள்ள வேண்டும்.

4. Akanksha Shukla

Strength in Women's Simplicity

In the quiet grace of her morning rise,
She carries worlds within her eyes.
A woman strong, yet soft as rain,
In silence, she endures the strain.

No roaring words, no battle shout,
Her power whispers, never doubt.
For in her smile, calm and pure,
Lies a strength that will endure.

She builds her life with steady hands,
No need for crowns or grand demands.
Her soul a river, flowing wide,
In her simplicity, strength can't hide.

Through every storm, she'll stand her ground,
With feet firm, but heart unbound.
In every breath, her power grows—
A quiet force that always shows.

5. Nakul Rathi

"Tum sath raha karo, accha lagta hai...
Haq jatana tum par accha lagta hai...
Accha lagta hai tere sath mere zindagi ka har lamha bitana,
Mujhe tu behad accha lagta hai...

Accha lagta hai tumhe muskurana, aur mujhe tumhe muskurate dekhna accha lagta hai...
Tumse nazrein chura kar nazrein padhna accha lagta hai...
Tujhe kore kagaz par apne alfaz mein uttarna accha lagta hai...
Chand se tumhari baatein karna accha lagta hai...
Accha lagta hai tera mujhe samjhana...
Accha lagta hai tere aansu ban kar khud beh jana...
Accha lagta hai tune ki hui har baat dohrana...
Accha lagta hai tujhe har baat par satana...
Accha lagta hai tumhe mere har geet mein gana...

Kaise bataun, bas accha lagta hai tumse bina baat ke dil lagana...

(Loving you for no reason is the job I use to love)"

6. આયુષ અંધારીકર

તમને મળીને બચપણ મળી ગયું,
અમે તો જવાબદારીના બોજમાં દબાયેલા હતા.

તમને મળીને બાળપણ યાદ આવી ગયું,
અમે તો કોઈકના લીધે આ બધું જ ખોઈ બેઠા હતા.

તમને મળીને નાના થઈ શકાયું,
અમે તો ક્યારનાય મોટા થઈ ગયા હતા.

તમને મળીને નાના બાળની રોઈ શકાયું,
અમે તો આંસુ છુપાવતા થઈ ગયા હતા.

તમને મળીને અમે ફરી બચ્ચા જેવી જીદ કરતા થયા,
અમે તો ઘણા સમજદાર થઈ ગયા હતા

7. Harsh M. Joshi

HEROES

It takes great strength to train
To modern service your ancestral brain ;
To lift the weight Of the unnumbered years
Of dead men's habits , methods ,and ideas ;
To hold that back with one hand, and support
With the other the weak steps Of the new thought .
It takes great strength to bring your life up square
With your accepted thought and hold it there ;
Resisting the inertia that drags back
From new attempts to the Old habit 's track.
It is so easy to drift back, to sink ;
So hard to live abreast Of what you
think.
It takes great strength to live where you belong
When other people think that you are wrong ;
People you love , and who love you, and whose
Approval is a pleasure you would choose .
To bear this pressure a n d succeed at length
In living your belief— well , it takes strength,
And courage , too . But what does courage mean
Save strength to help you face a pain
Foreseen Courage to undertake this lifelong strain
Of setting yours against your grand sire 's brain ;
Dangerous risk o f walking lone
Out Of the easy paths that used to be ,
An d the fierce pain of hurting those we love
When love meets truth, and truth must ride above .
But the best courage man has ever shown
Is daring to cu t loose an d think alone .
Dark are the unlit chambers Of clear space
Where light shines back from no reflecting face .
Our sun's wide glare , our heaven's
shining blue , We owe to fog and dust they fumble through ;
And our rich wisdom that we treasure so

Shines from the thousand things that we don't know.
But to think new— it takes a courage grim
As led Columbus over the world's rim .
To think it cost some courage . And to go
Try it . It takes every power you know.
It takes great love to stir the human heart
To live beyond the others and apart .
A love that is n ot shallow, is not small ,
Is not for on e or two , but for them all .
Love that c an wound love for its higher need ;
Love that can leave love , though the heart may bleed ;
Love that c an lose love , family and friend,
Yet steadfastly live , loving, to the end.
A love that asks no answer, that can live
Moved by on e burning, deathless force— to give .
Love , strength, and courage strength, and love .
The heroes of all time are built thereof.

8. Muskaan

सवाल-ए-मोहब्बत

दिल में बेतुक़ा सा ख़याल आया है,
पूछूं क्या जो ये सवाल आया है..?

रूठोगे तो नहीं तुम अगर मलाल आया है,
पूछूं क्या जो ये सवाल आया है..?

बार-बार मुझमें बेमिसाल आया है,
पूछूं क्या जो ये सवाल आया है..?

उम्मीद तो है अगर ये तेरे नाल आया है,
पूछूं क्या जो ये सवाल आया है..?

निगाहों में अक्सर जो धुंधला हाल आया है,
पूछूं क्या जो ये सवाल आया है..?

दिल की गलियों में एक बेपरवाह बेहाल आया है,
पूछूं क्या जो ये सवाल आया है..?

वक़्त की रफ़्तार में कुछ अंजाम सा जाल गया,
पूछूं क्या जो ये सवाल आया है..?

हर धड़कन में तेरी यादों का जमाल आया है,
पूछूं क्या जो ये सवाल आया है..?

शायद मोहब्बत का नया एक साल आया है,
पूछूं क्या जो ये सवाल आया है..?

9. Ishita Verma

वो कौन थी ??

प्रेम अगन में पक रही, नवयौवन छलकाए ।
एक झलक ही देखा बस , मुंह से निकला हाय ।।
कैसे कोई हो सकता है, इतना हॉट & स्वीट ।
पहुंच ही गया पास उसके , ये मन बनके ढीट ॥
कंपकंपे हाथों में जकड़ , लिया अधर से लगाये ।
कौन है यारो नाम उसका दू, कैसे तुम्हे बताए ।।
अधरो से चिपकी रही , वो हॉटी सी यार ।
जाने कैसे हो गया , उस सांवली से प्यार ॥
सुबह , पहर या शाम हो , उस बिन कटे ना हाय ।
नस नस में यूं समा गई , अब ना कुछ भी भाए ।।
आखिरी बूंद में तक ना मिला , दिल को मेरे संतोष ।
छा गई ऐसे दिल पे मेरे , दिखे ना कोई दोष ॥
चाहे दिल हरपल उसे , रात हो पहर या भोर ।
चुराके मेरा दिल ले गई , बनकरके चितचोर ॥
देहरादून की गन हिल पे , मिली वो मुझको हाय ।
गलत ना सोचो यारो वो है , कुल्हड़ वाली चाय ।।

10. Bhuvi Gajja

Smiling with friends, but lonely inside,
Hiding the tears that I cannot cry.
So many problems, none seem big enough,
To let my tears fall, to let out my stuff.
They tell me be brave, don't show your pain,
But holding it in drives me insane.
Happy outside, but torn deep within,
Fighting a battle I can't seem to win.
People's hopes weigh heavy on my soul,
Their words echo, taking a toll.
I want to break down, let the tears flow,
But I'm scared if I start, they'll never go.
So I keep it inside, play the part,
With a heavy mind and a weary heart.
In a world that tells me to always be tough,
I wish they'd see that I've had enough.
Tired of the fight, yet pushing each day,
I hold on tight, finding my way.
For even in pain, there's strength to be found,
In the quiet moments, without a sound.

11. Ms Nikhlesh Jaikishan Sejwar

आसान नहीं होता एक लड़की होना..
दूसरों के लिए अपना अस्तित्व खोना..
सर बुलंदी छूते हौसले मार कर सोना..
आसान नहीं होता एक लड़की होना |

कभी खुद टूट रोना पड़ता है..
कभी दिल के अरमान आंसुओ में भर तकिया भिगोना पड़ता है..
कभी इज्ज़त के नाम पर अभिलाषाओ को डुबोना पड़ता है..
मुश्किल होता है अपनी आंखों में दूसरों के सपने सजोना..
आसान नहीं होता एक लड़की होना ||

इतने साल जन्म ले एक जिंदगी जीना..
और फिर दूसरे घर जा, नए जीवन के धागे मे उम्मीद के मोती पिरोना..
रिश्तों के लिए अपनी सोच को बदलना पड़ता है..
लड़की होने का हर फर्ज अदा करना पड़ता है|

आसान नहीं होता एक लड़की होना..
रिश्तों के लिए अपनी पहचान अपना अस्तित्व खोना |

बहता है खून और खुशियां मनाईं जाती हैं,
हमारी बेटी वंश बढ़ाने लायक हो गयी है,
कुछ इस तरह बात बताई जाती है,
है उस बहते हुए सुर्ख लाल रंग से वंश महफूस ,
क्या कभी कर सकते हो उस दर्द के एहसास को महसूस ?
बेआराम कैसे वो खुद को पाती है ,
पर किसी को बताने में हिचकिचाती है,

आसान नहीं होता एक लड़की होना..
रिश्तों के लिए अपनी पहचान अपना अस्तित्व खोना |

उसके लिए उन दिनों क्यों मंदिर मस्जिद के कपाट अवरुद्ध है,
जन्म यही देती हैं तो क्यों ऐसे समय में समाज उनके विरुद्ध है?
दुनिया बनाने वाली माँ के जब तुम भक्त हो,
तो जन्म देने वाली माँ के लिए कैसे इतने सख्त हो?
क्यों ऐसे तिरस्कृत किया जाता है,

क्यों खाना तक दूर से खिसका दिया जाता है?
क्यों उस पीड़ा को नज़र अंदाज कर दिया जाता है?
ये ख़्याल मन को झंझोर जाता है,ये ख़्याल बार बार मन में आता है|

आसान नहीं होता एक लड़की होना..
रिश्तों के लिए अपनी पहचान अपना अस्तित्व खोना |

12. Pranav Sheth

Never Stop Learning and Upskill Yourself

न चोरहायन च राजहाय, न ○तभा यन च भारकार । ययकत
वधतएव नय, वयाधनसवधन धानम॥

na cauhāryam na ca rājahāryam, na bhrāt bhājyam
na ca bhārakāril vyaye krte vardhata eva nityam,
Vidyādhanam sarvadhanapradhānamil

Translation- That which cannot be stolen by a thief, That which cannot be summoned by a king. That which cannot be divided between siblings as heirloom, That which is not a heavy burden to carry around, That which grows when shared, That is the wealth of knowledge, which is the supreme of all material wealth.

Asimple truth of life- "Knowledge is never Ending" Warren Buffett, known for his success as an investor and as a businessman, has emphasized the importance of constant learning and upskilling. One famous example of Warren Buffett upskilling himself is his focus on understanding technology.

In the early 2000s, Warren Buffett admitted that he had made a mistake by not investing in technology companies during the dot-com boom. To rectify this, he started to understand the tech industry. In 2011, Berkshire Hathaway, Warren Buffett's company, made an investment in IBM. Warren Buffett acknowledged that he needed to adapt to the modern changing business model and understand the role of technology. By investing in a technology company (IBM) and staying informed about advancements in the tech sector.

This example shows Warren Buffett's willingness to learn, evolve, and apply new knowledge to his investment approach, showcasing the importance of continuous learning and adaptation in the business world.

If you would have done masters in Machine Learning in 2020 you would not know so much about Artificial Intelligence (AI) but if you want to work today at a good position, in a good firm, with a good package you need to learn everything about AI because you need to be skilled, you need to be an Asset for your company and not a liability. There is something new everyday and you should be updated with it.

Learning is not just limited to a classroom or a specific period of life; it is a lifelong journey that shapes our minds, enhances our skills and revises our previous knowledge. From the moment we are born, we are natural learners. Lifelong learning is essential for staying competitive in the corporate world. With the rapid change in technology, many industries are constantly evolving, and the skills that were in demand yesterday may become obsolete tomorrow. To remain up to date you need to invest time and money in acquiring new skills as soon as they are in the market.

Learning is not just limited to educational schools and universities, it is beyond it. In today's digital era, knowledge is available for free or with cheap fees like Online courses, webinars, podcasts, videos and books. To keep on learning, first you need to remove the orthodox thinking that tells you to stop learning after graduation. If you don't learn you are not going to be in the competition of the corporate world, someone else is going to take your position and be successful.

Next, you need to learn to adapt and change, if you don't, your story or journey ends there like it happened to KODAK, one of the best camera making companies in the world. Other companies evolved and started making digital cameras but KODAK was not able to adapt to fast changing market conditions. The company was focused on protecting its original existing business, rather than adapting to new technologies and opportunities. As a result, Kodak was left behind as the photography industry shifted towards digital.

So, learn to adapt to the surrounding world and start executing by learning new things and skills.

Skills are things which will help you be at a high post in MNCsand earn a lot of money. You should always spend some of your time learning something new, like if you are a teenager you can learn Coding Languages, Photography, Video Editing, Graphic Designing, SEO Marketing, etc. . For Example, if there are two people A and B. A upskills in Graphic Designing, Video Editing, Coding and many other things and B only hold a degree then the chance of A getting a job will be higher as for doing work you need practical (Hard) skills and not necessarily a degree without

practical skills.
You don't really need to pay every time for upskilling, you can just learn from YouTube Videos, Podcasts and Blogs. If you are willing for certificates you could do professional courses on Udemy, Coursera, Google Courses and Many others, it could be a part of your resume.

When you start upskilling yourself, make a plan or timeline to follow for learning. You should not just study theory but also do it practically. Don't spend your whole time upskilling yourself because academics are very crucial in High School. Keep a schedule everyday for upskilling.

Now you know what Hard Skills are but do you know what Soft Skills are? Of Course it's not like a teddy like hard teddy and soft teddy. Soft skills are skills which help you present your hard skills to others, soft skills give an additional magic help to your hard skills as it is the way you present, express and communicate yourself.

"Your hard skills help you acquire employment and your soft skills help you ensure your employability. Hence, integrate hard and soft skills to fast-track your career."-Professor M.S. Rao

Howto turn Mobile from Distraction to Helping Hand

There are so many apps in the market which help freelancers to earn money online by showcasing their skills and working for companies and influencers. Some of them are Fiverr, Funngro and many more. It can help you earn your pocket money.

13. Achyut Umarji

।। श्रीकृष्ण ।।

पहिली शिवी खाऊंनही...
नव्याण्णव शिव्या ऐकण्याचे... सामर्थ्य आहे...
तो कृष्ण आहे...।।१।।

सुदर्शन चक्रासारखा अस्त्र
असूनही...
ज्यांच्या हातात नेहमी बासरी असावी...
तो कृष्ण आहे... ।।२।।

द्वारिका सारखं वैभव असताना...
सुदामा सारखा मित्र असावा...
तो कृष्ण आहे...।।३।।

मृत्यु समोर असताना...
कालिया मर्दनच्या फनावर नाचावं...
तो कृष्ण आहे...।।४।।

सर्वसामार्थ्य असताना...
पण युध्दात सारथीची भूमिका बजावणारा...
तो कृष्ण आहे...।।५।।

श्रीकृष्ण जन्माष्टमीच्या हार्दिक शुभेच्छा।।

अच्युत उमर्जी

14. Anjali Jain

Nakodaji the jain tirth

Nakoda ji tirth is a beautiful jain tirth which touches everyone's heart at first go. If we say this place jannat it's not wrong. At NAKODAJI there's a mela of Sunday and poornima of every month. Nakoda Dham is always as beautiful as nothing in the world. If a person goes there once he will be habited to go NAKODAJI Dham. There's a mela of parshvnath bhagwan is in December or January Posh Dasami when Parasnath bhagwan was born. And a mela in February or that's magh sudi teras. Nakodaji the jain tirth is situated in Balotra Barmer Rajasthan. Nearest railway station Balotra Nearest Airport jodhpur.

This site is primarily dedicated to Lord Parshvanath, who is worshipped here as Nakoda Bhairav.

The glory of Nakodaji Tirth is not only in its antiquity and architecture but also in the divinity and religious atmosphere it offers. Devotees come from far and wide to fulfill their wishes here. It is believed that by the grace of Nakoda Bhairav, any obstacles and problems in life are removed.

The architecture of Nakodaji Temple is marvelous, built in the traditional Rajasthani style. The sanctum houses a beautiful idol of Lord Parshvanath. The idol of Nakoda Bhairav is also a central figure of deep faith for devotees. Upon entering the temple premises, one immediately experiences a unique peace and positive energy.

Every devotee who comes here is filled with immense faith and belief. People bow their heads here, praying for solutions to their life's problems, and they experience the greatness of Nakoda Bhairav. The natural beauty and serene environment surrounding the temple provide mental peace and spiritual tranquility.

Nakodaji is not just a religious site but also a medium for spiritual purification for devotees. Visiting this sacred place is considered an important religious duty for every Jain follower.

This pilgrimage site has earned a permanent place in the hearts of its devotees, and the glory of Nakoda Bhairav will continue to resonate throughout the ages.

15. Delisha

DEAD LIGHT SWITCH
You peer out at me
Broken and useless,Naked and ugly

Void of life
Once
Lightning coursed through your copper veins. No more

We stare
Face to face
I don't see you. You are just
Part of our rough - cut trailer walls

You embody our hand -me-down house
Cracking and old striken with mold
You
Are the house.you ,are all we can get

You
Don't matter .you don't matter.because
Our light does not come from switch
Because we
Don't get our light from some switch because we get our light from each other

16. Shria Chirvi

Strangers to best friends

We started off as strangers, two worlds apart,
Who knew you'd end up stealing a piece of my heart?
You were calm, I was chaos, like night and day,
But somehow, our bond found its way.

From 'dewar' to 'ex-dewar,' what a wild ride,
Yet through it all, you stood by my side.
Our conversations? Well, they make zero sense,
But somehow, they make my world feel a little less tense.

You annoy me, I scold you—what a game,
Yet every time, we walk away the same.
I cry, and there you are, with your warmth and care,
Turning my tears into laughter, like magic in the air.

You're my gossip buddy, my partner in crime,
Even when you're wrong, somehow you're right every time!
I never thought you'd mean this much to me,
But look at us now, like a crazy, loving part of family.

You challenge me, and I challenge you,
But what stays strong is the bond that's true.
You're the brother I never knew I'd find,
In your silly ways, I found peace of mind.

So here's to you, the one who makes me mad and laugh,
Who can annoy me and still be my better half.
I love you more than words can say,
And I thank the universe every single day.

For turning a stranger into my brother so tight,
Someone who brings both madness and light.
So here's a poem, filled with tears and cheer,
Because, my dear brother, you're my forever here.

17. Santhoshi Choradia

CEREMONY OF NAVRATRI: A FIERY TRIBUTE TO "YAGYASENI"

Doesn't Our glam face looks patchy?
In the absence of Smile and Makeup,
Likewise, this "Sharad navratri" wouldn't be flashy,
Alfresco! Colorful Rangoli, Dandiya, Garba, the reverence of Ten Goddess and the Sacred water in Glub,

Thy "amigos", "amigas" y "Vecinos" of India, Srilanka, Singapore, Malaysia, Mauritius, South Africa and Reunion,
Let's "burn the midnight oil", to "sparkle" over the Mansarovar river, for the incarnation of "Sachi", "Nalayini" and "Celestial Sri", as One,

The Indian epic fire-born woman of "Substance" and "Enamour", with dark Complexion, "lotus" eyes, "blue and Curly" locks,
Or Should we call her, "Draupadi", a paragon of Gender and resistance, "being in the doghouse" humiliated by Duryodhan and Disrobed by Dushashan, in the courts of Gauravas and saved by the "lord Krishna", by granting the lengthiest saree, infront of the flocks?

18. Rakesh Kumar Singh

चाँदनी रात है और मौसम हँसी
    तुम्हें याद कर दिल मचलने लगा।
मेरी आँखों में तुम हो समाए हुए
    तुम्हारे बिना दम निकलने लगा।

आपको देख लूँ तो करार आये हैं
    जैसे मौसम में फिर से बाहर आये हैं।
मुझपे जादू किया आपने दिलरुबा
    तुम्हारे बिना दिल तड़पने लगा।

खुशबू तुम्हारे बदन के सनम
    नहीं भूल पाया तुम्हारी कसम।
आपका साथ हमको मिले हमनवा,
    अपनी चाहत का मधुरस बरसने लगा।

कारे कजरारे नैना नशीले तेरे
    चैन दिल का चुरा कर गए हैं मेरे।
जुल्फें तुम्हारी है जैसे घटा,
    दीप यादों का हर पल है जलने लगा।

आपका सारा अंदाज प्यारा लगे,
    सारी दुनिया से हमको है न्यारा लगे।
जिंदगी हो मेरी बंदगी को मेरी,
    अपनी चाहत का प्याला छलकने लगा।

19. Akira Sravani

The Cry For Justice

Khushi Amara Ray is a beautiful and kind witch. She belongs to the Sacred Coven.

She is standing in front of Durga Maa statue in her house. "Hey Dyrga Maa. Today is the start of Navratri. And this year's celebrations are going to be indeed hell for the culprits who dared to torment women, who dared to disrespect women. This time you are going to break our fast by serving us the feast in the form of punishing our culprit and giving us the needed justice in best as a safe tomorrow. We hope you will hear our loud cry in this war and allow the truth to win."

Thus, hoping for a safe tomorrow Khushi today started Navratri for justice.

20. उमेश कुमारी "प्रेरणा"

क़िस्मत की दरारों को सलीक़े से भरती है औरत,
हर दर्द-ए-जहाँ को अपने दिल में रखती है औरत।

तूफ़ानों की रहगुज़र में चट्टान सी हो जाती है,
ज़ुल्मात के साये में भी चराग़ जलाती है औरत।

तल्ख़ियों से न डरे, हौसला बेशुमार उसका,
हर ख़्वाब को हक़ीक़त में बदल कर दिखाती है औरत।

जज़्बात की चुप्पियों में लिपटी रहती है अक्सर,
अश्क़ों को दुआओं में छुपा के हँसती है औरत।

अज़्म बन के, हर फ़िक्र को गले से लगाती,
अपने ही वजूद से इन्क़लाब लाती है औरत।

21. Dr. Sree Varshini R

Title: Let Me Flow for You
Author: Dr. Sree Varshini R
Genre: Poem

Let me flow for you, like a river wide,
Through valleys deep, where secrets hide.
I'll carry your dreams on gentle waves,
And wash away the fear that enslaves.

Let me flow for you, like a breeze so light,
Through every storm, through day and night.
I'll whisper hope in each passing sigh,
And lift your heart to touch the sky.

Let me flow for you, with love so pure,
A bond unbroken, strong and sure.
Through every path, I'll guide you true,
Just let me flow—for you, I'll do.

22. Archita Mohanty

When a Villain Fell in Love

In shadows deep, where darkness lay,
A heart once cold, began to sway.
No light had touched the path he trod,
Yet in her eyes, he glimpsed a god.

With hands that shaped the cruelest fate,
He dared to dream, though much too late.
The world he ruled with iron fist,
Was shattered by her gentle kiss.

Her laughter echoed, soft and sweet,
In places where no joy could meet.
And though he fought the love's command,
He found her warmth slipped through his hand.

The villain's heart, long wrapped in chains,
Now beat with love, but filled with pains.
For in her gaze, he saw the truth—
He'd never be her hero's youth.

Yet still he loved, in silence stayed,
A villain bound, by love betrayed.
For even shadows long to see,
A world where love might set them free.

But love, for him, was never kind—
A fleeting dream that slipped his mind.
He watched her fade into the night,
And lost himself to endless plight.

23. Selva Mahalakshmi S (Agni)

Title: Nature and the Purpose of Life

Sunlight hit my face through the window, I wake up
As I open the window, cold breeze kiss my cheeks
Morning bliss gives a good vibes.
Dew drops are shining like pearls on meadow
Buds are blooming and spread its fragrance,
Which send as an invitation to bugs and butterfly to celebrate the birthday of flowers.
Each visitor got honey as birthday sweet. As cold breeze continue it's rhythm
Dandelions are dancing back - and - forth Spreading seeds in air and then it become rich fertilizer.
Birth and death took place at the same time
How beautifully nature teaches a life lesson!

We are born on earth
Dancing as much as we want
Strings are pulled by almighty;
making us to put perfect steps for rhythm Then extend our generation
At last become a good fertilizer for soil. Even life is in a size of Pinky finger,
Wasting time in using index finger to criticize others .
Having space in ring finger and dream for someone who not even exist as per our expectations.
But purpose of our actual life is far from these things ,
Where nature is the key to find it.
Let your soul wander around the mother nature .

24. Asgar Hussain

Whispers of Tomorrow

The stars once whispered secrets to me,
Of dreams that dance, wild and free.
In the quiet of the night's soft glow,
They spoke of places I'd someday go.

The winds carried stories from afar,
Of courage shining like the brightest star.
With every breath, a tale was spun,
Of battles lost, and battles won.

The river sang with ancient grace,
Reflecting journeys time can't erase.
In its depths, I saw a spark,
A flame to guide me through the dark.

Tomorrow waits with open arms,
With joys unknown and unseen charms.
So I'll walk forward, step by step,
Trusting the promises that fate has kept.

For life is a poem, verse by verse,
A treasure we both own and rehearse.
And in the whispers of night's embrace,
I'll find my path, my sacred place.

25. Manju Preetham Kuntamukkala

చిట్టి బొజ్జ గణపయ్య
నిన్ను తలచినానయ్య
కుడుములు ఉండ్రాళ్లు
చేసితి నికే భారము అనుకోకయ్య
లాగించవయ్యా బుజ్జి గణపయ్య

తోరపు తొండము తోడ
తర్జన భర్జన పడక
వంట ఘుమ ఘుమలు
ఆరగిస్తు మమ్ము కావుము
చిన్ని గణపయ్య

ఆశల నడుమ పరుగులు తీసే
జీవ ప్రాణులం మేము
విఘ్నములు రానియక కాచుము
మమ్ము, నిన్ను నదిలో కలిపెదము

స్వార్థ ప్రయోజనాల కోసమే
అలవడిన మేము
నీ పేరు చెప్పి పర్యవరణమునే కలుషితం
చేసెదము
అన్నీ ఒర్చి నీ బింబం ముందే నాట్యములు
చేసి అలరించి గెలుచుదుము శబ్దభేరి

మ్రొక్కెదము మ్రొక్కెదము మేము
నిండుగా మెండుగా నిన్నే గణపయ్య
గుణములు లేని బ్రతుకులు అవుతున్నా
విలువంటూ కోల్పోతున్న పండగ ఘనముగా
చేసెదము నీకే ఓ గణపయ్య .....!

మాకు బుద్ధిని ఇచ్చి
బుజ్జి జ్ఞానము కలిగించి
సమాజ హితం కోరే మనుషులను చేసి
ఆటంకములు తొలగించి
నీ నిండు చూపులు కురిపించి
మా మహనీయ కార్యములు జయములు చేయించి

సహాయ హృదయమును ఇచ్చి
మలినములు ఉన్న మనస్సును అదుపు చేసి
నిర్విఘ్న గమనము ఏర్పరచి
మమ్ము కావుము విఘ్నరాజా ఎల్లవేళలా...!

26. ROHIT RATAN KHAIRNAR

वडिलांची माया

बाप या शब्दांत सगळ्या गोष्टी सामावते
बाप या शब्दांत मुलीची व्यथा स्पष्ट होते
बाप या शब्दांत त्याच्या कष्टाची उणीव कळते
बाप या शब्दांत त्याने केलेल्या प्रयत्नांना यश मिळते

बाप हा मुलीची ढाल आहे
बाप हा मुलांचा आधारस्तंभ आहे
बाप हा कुटुंबाचा पाया आहे
बाप हा लेकरांचा सहारा आहे

बाप माझा सखासांगाती आहे
बाप माझा धैर्यशील आहे
बाप हा दुःख सांगत नसतो
बाप हा आनंद साजरा कधीच करत नसतो

बाप हा बघायचा आहे तर फाटक्या ड्रेस मध्ये बघा
बाप हा बघायचा आहे तर त्याने कोणत्या गोष्टीशी झगडलेला आहे ते बघा
बाप हा बघायचा आहे तर त्याने कुटुंबामागे घेतलेले कष्ट बघ
बाप हा बघायचा आहे तर तुमच्या बरोबर कायम खंबीर नेतृत्व जो असतो तो म्हणजे बाप

बाप हा मुलाची सावली आहे
बाप हा मुलीची माऊली आहे
लग्राच्या वेळी ढसाढसा रडतो तो म्हणजे बाप
कन्यादान जो करतो तो म्हणजे बाप

रोहित रतन खैरनार

27. DEEPAK BARAI

मैं खुद के दुख से रूबरू नहीं हो पा रहा,
यह क्या कसमोकस है कि रो भी नहीं पा रहा ।

खुद को तो काफी दूर कर दिया है मैंने तुमसे,
फिर भी मैं तुम्हें भूल क्यूँ नहीं पा रहा ।

तुम्हें तकलीफ न हो इसलिए ही तो मैं दूर हूँ,
मेरा दिल शायद इसलिए भी कहीं लग नहीं पा रहा ।

हाँ मोहब्बत आज भी है तुमसे और शायद पहले से भी ज्यादा,
पर कैसा यह डर है कि इश्क बयाँ भी नहीं कर पा रहा ।

लोगों को तो समझा दिया है कि दूर हो गया हूँ तुम्हारी यादों से भी,
पर क्या पता नहीं यह बात मैं खुद को समझा नहीं पा रहा.

बात क्या अब तो तुम्हें देखने को भी तरस गए हैं,
कोई डर है या है नफरत हमसे यह बात भी मैं समझ नहीं पा रहा ।

माँ की गोद में सिर रख तो दिया है लेकिन,
क्या दुख है मुझे यह माँ से कह भी नहीं पा रहा ।
-Deepak Barai.

28. TARIQ AZAM KASHMIRI

poem.when i met myself
When i met myself.....
In an old broken mirror of my room
I saw....
THE dreams were shrinked
In the frozen Heart
And the innocent emotions
Were hanging in the eyes
when i met myself
In the Desert Of life
i saw....
The dune of memories
were scattered in grains
Then wind blowed them
Here to there and there to anywhere
when i met myself
on the brink of the ocean
i saw....
in the middle of it
The boat of life were jolting
by the tides of worries
And an angry whirlpool swallowed it
when i met myself
in an old folded diary
i saw...
from eyes of the stories
The River of tears was flowing
clamly and steadly....
when i met myeslf
every where in this way
i take steps back to
where i will not meet myself again
by Tariq azam Kashmiri

29. Suresh Kannan Nadar

"மானிடம் போற்றும் மகாத்மா"

தேசத் தந்தையே,

உன்னை
மகத்துவமாய் பார்த்தோம்,
மகிமையாய் பார்த்தோம்,
மதிப்பாய் பார்த்தோம்.

உன்னையே
காற்றாய் பார்த்தோம்,
காவியமாய் பார்த்தோம்,
காசாய் பார்த்தோம்.

உன்னையோ
புத்தகமாய் பார்த்தோம்,
சத்தியமாய் பார்த்தோம்,
அர்த்தமாய் பார்த்தோம்.

உன்னைத்தான்
மாற்றமாய் பார்த்தோம்,
மாண்பாய் பார்த்தோம்,
மாமனிதராய் பார்த்தோம்.

மொத்தத்தில் உன்னை
மகாத்மாவாய் பார்த்தோம்.

30. Prerana Gavhande

तुम कवल सी भोर भाती
मे शाम सा ढलता सूरज प्रिये
केश जैसे कोई लेहरती सरिता
मैं गंगा का घाट कोई
माथे पे तकदिर की लकिरे
जीसपे मे खुद को देखु
कर्ण जणू पीपल की पल्लवी
मेरा आवाज उनमे कैद प्रिये
नयन जैसे कोई मीनाक्षी हो
मे उसमे धुंद सी छवी
लब मानो गुलाब की पंखुडिया
मे उसका सुगंध प्रिये
अलंकारो के बिना भी गला खूब निखरता है
उसे देख हर बार मेरा मन फिसलता है
हाथ जैसे छोटी सी पेडो की डालीया
मे छोटा सा कतरा हू
पैर जणू खीले हुवे पुष्प
मैं इर्धगिर्ध भटकता भवरा प्रिये
ये अलौकिक येशवर्य मुझे भ्रमित करता है
जैसे तुम कोई मन मोहिनी प्रिये
बन जाव इस मन की अधिकारिका
मे सदा बन के रहु तुम्हारा दास प्रिये
सरल सा पेहनावा ये आंतारिक सौंदर्य
मुझे हर बार खेच लेता है
फिर खुद ही देखता हू अर्पण मे
मेरा मन रोक लेता है
तुम सबको भानेवाली मनपसंद कुमारिका
मैं आम सा एकतर्फा आशिक प्रिये!

31. AKASH MONDAL

Echoes Of Tomorrow

In the dawn of world reborn,
Where stars whisper secrets to the sea,
The echoes of tomorrow are born,
In the heartbeats of eternity.
Skies painted with dreams untold,
Where the sun and moon embrace,
A tapestry of stories unfold,
In the cosmic dance of time and space.
Mountains hum ancient songs,
As rivers carve their paths anew,
In the silence where the earth belongs,
A future blooms in every dew.
Voices of the past linger near,
In the winds that shape our fate,
But the echoes of tomorrow we hear,
Are the dreams we dare to create.
So rise with the dawn, hearts alight,
Let your soul be the guiding star,
For in the echoes of tomorrow's night,
We find the truth of who we are.

32. Archana

A Ordinary life

The real beauty of life about understanding every situation. For every innings we no need to be prepared or practiced atleast we should have the courage to face the situation. The problems are happening by the firm believe of the solution so we should tackle , we can tackle ,we will tackle with our hope best of luck to face your own perspectives!!

33. Pragya

Scene 1
Voice 1
I saw,………. saw the fire, the fire that was burning around. It was killing………. something. I could feel it but…
Another voice interrupts
But what?????
Impatience Another the voice
Voice 1
I don't know it just…….. there something but ….. I am unable to connect . I want focus on this. I see myself as a bestselling author. But you guys!!!
Simply ignoring earlier said words Voice 2
Leave all of this you know that we have so much too do. So much is pending. And here you are sitting idle. Just get up. And please get a job okay you are thirty now. You have to settle down also.This hobby of yours will ruin you one day
Voice 1
This is not just hobby but my passion and if it demands my ruins then in second less than one shall I surrender

…
Scene 2
A book launch event
Author
hello everyone this is my novel, a novel that I have been working on for years. Please give this a chance.
Reader 1
Hey isn't this the author who spoke about how the new laws may cause more damage then help.
Reader 2
Yes he is the one. But look what he is writing trashy romance novel. Now you understand why people say one should stick to there job.

The author thinks from the background and accepts that he might have not spoken out loud but look at his books. The are the love spectre of my dilemma and pain. But they are right too they have not seen me struggling.

….
Scene 3
A book store

Readice Publication

Assistant
Hello mam what are looking for today?
Reader
Hello I am not much into fiction. I would like to explore something in that .
Assistant
Sure mam this is one of the novel that has been recently published by a very renowned author. It's about some political conflicts of the society.
Reader
But isn't this the same author who has sedition charges against him? No no I am not interested. I am a nationalist. I believe she should die.

Suddenly news channel starts screaming
The writing walking by the streat was shot dead
….

34. Sukriti Yadav

विषय:- लुप्त प्रेमियो की प्रजाति ...

शायद लुप्त हो गई वो प्रेमियो की प्रजाति,
जो अपनी प्रेमिकाओ को घर की बहू बनाया करते थे।
देखते बहुत से स्वप्न,
उनमें से कुछ पूर्ण होने की अभिलाषा करते थे।
लिव-इन-रिलेशनशिप था ना तब,
बस प्रेमिका की एक झलक देखने को मचलते थे।
कनक-रजत का तो कोई दौर ही ना था,
वो बजार से झुमके दिलाता था।
तब ये इंटरनेट का जमाना ना था,
वो लैंडलाइन से कॉल कर,
प्रेमिका की आवाज(हम्म) सुनता था।
बिना किसी काम के वो,
रास्ता तय किया करता था।
ब्यूटी पार्लर का जमाना ना था,
वो लाली और बिंदी दिया करता था।
प्रेमिका भी सज-सवरकर आती थी,
मानो जैसे कोई प्रेम की रसम निभाती थी।
हाथो मे चूड़ी,पैर मैं पायल लाती थी,
कुछ इस तरह वो अपनी उपस्थिति का अनुभव कराती थी।
श्रृंगार के नाम पर वो,
केशो पर गजरा
आँखों में काजल
छोटी सी बिंदी
हल्की सी लाली
कानो में झुमके
और सिर पर चुन्नी लाती थी।
प्रेमी के नज़र मिलाते ही वो कुम्हला सी जाती थी,
कुछ इस तरह वो प्रेमिका से पत्नी बन जाती थी।
प्रेमिका के दर्श मात्र से ही वो सहम से जाते थे,
अपने बालो पर हाथ फेर हल्का सा मुस्कुरा जाते थे।

35. AK Dhiman 'Veer'

शीर्षक –: मेरे आगोश में

ऐसी सर्द रातों में वो मेरे आगोश में हो
सुनाई दें सिर्फ़ धड़कनें दो दिलों की
सर्द रातों में गर्म साँसें खामोश सी हों

अब मेरा हुस्न–ए–चाँद भी शर्मा जाए
कि तुम मेरे लिए उस गर्म लिबास सी हो
जिसमें सिमटकर मेरी रूह गरमा जाए

दस्तूर–ए–ऐलान करने से न डरें हम
न ही ये सर्द रातें हमें खफ़ा कर जाएँ
दो दिलों को मिला दे ज़माने का ज़म।।

ज़म –: इसके मायने हैं जोड़ना, इकट्ठे होना, जोड़ कर रखना।

36. Ramya N

மரணம்

அறியாத வயதில் விட்டு சென்றாய்..
அறியும் முன்னே விலகிச் சென்றாய்..
கண் முன்னே படுத்து கிடந்தாய்..
விவரம் தெரிந்து விட்டு பிரிந்தாய்.. அழைத்தும் எலாமல்இருந்தாய்..
அனைவரும் வாழும்படி சேர்த்து வைத்தாய்..
கூடவே இருப்பதாய் எண்ணிக் கொண்டு வாழ்கிறேன் என் அப்பா..

37. UTKARSHAA SINGH

DAUGHTER'S ARRIVAL

In silence for ages, today I break it free,
Breaking down all doors, today truth shall be.

Never consider my patience as my weakness, if you may,
A pain like a mountain, how long can I stay?

Today, I demand answers to my questions,
Revealing the pain of countless past sessions.

Why was there mourning when SHE was born,
A daughter's arrival, a face forlorn.

Abusing new mother, they made her weep,
Because the heir wasn't a son, troubles ran deep.

Throwing her in the dustbin, they couldn't find shame,
When dogs attacked, how loudly she exclaimed.

Thrown in bushes, in dirty drains,
Her arrival wasn't welcomed, only strains.

Surviving the doctor's knife from the start,
Now every day, a new death in this world's chart.

Surviving pain, a lesson learned from birth,
Our treatment is similar to animals on Earth.

Shackles upon us since childhood,
Every eye inside and outside home,
a hunter in the woods.

Daughter, don't go here, daughter, don't eat this,
This is not how you walk, this is not what you dress.

Don't laugh loudly, listen carefully,
You are PARAYA DHAN , a burden on our family.

Drowning in poison every person we meet,
Our war will continue until daughters are secure, concrete.

When drums play at a daughter's arrival,

Blessings will be given, and songs will rival.

BETI BACHAO BETI PADHAO , the slogan when come true,
On that day, our all efforts will be through.

38. Shaikh Shahajad Ahmad

"Screams of Love"

A friend unique, unlike any other,
Heals wounds like cells, and tissue cover.
A diary in flesh and bone,
Holds every emotion, every tone.

Indirect whispers of love's refrain,
Like trees in the forest, love sustains.
I, the fool, failed to divine,
Missed the signs, love's subtle design.

A clock of guilt, as she moved on,
Heart now weeps for the love that's gone.
Memories strikes, days turn dark,
Night becomes a haunting, sorrowful arc.

Every moment, facing your portrait,
Heart weeps, revealing love's regret.
Yes, I know you won't return,
Still, I'll linger, for love, I yearn.

:- Shaikh Shahajad Ahmad

39. Suraj Pandit

तू ही है जगपिता

जिसके अधीन है यह दुनिया,
अधीन है जिसके हम।
यह कल भी उसी के हाथ में,
हैं उसी के हम।
जिसके बिना यह संसार,
मात्र कल्पना सा है।
जिसके बिना हम अधूरे।

जिसने पयाल त्याग, हलाहल का पान किया,
जिसने एक इच्छा पर सब त्याग दिया।
अनेक हैं नाम उनके, अनेक हैं रूप,
तू ही है सहारा, तू ही है धूप।

तेरे बिना न कोई रूप, न कोई माया।
तू ही है जगपिता, तू ही है काया।
तू ही है धरती, तू ही है अंबर।
हम तेरे भक्त, तू ही शम्भू निराला।

इस सावन के शुभ दिन में,
तेरी उपस्थिति को महसूस कर रहा हूँ।
तेरे ही नाम पर हर कर्म कर रहा हूँ।

--------- सूरज पंडित

40. Manav Chopra

"What is Love?"

In the blank canvas of time her presence, a palette of hues, paints my existence, leaving my soul with resilience for existence, painted by a fragment of brilliance

She is not a possession I seek anymore nor do I seek the ownership of her love but a voyage through the time I share with her

For seeking her love would take away her freedom and love is not possession, it is the freedom of 2 hearts intertwining at their own will

For only one trapping the other, would leave scars of trying to let go

For I can never hurt her, so fragile and delicate

I yearn not to confine her but only let her soul free

From the chains of this cruel world who has trapped her for far too long

But In this garden of coexistence, selfishness somehow finds a way to bloom

I could have had all of her but the clocks were at the wrong junction of time

So I release the notion of owning her, like a bird from a gentle hand, all in the name of my love for her

For love is not about having all of her rather it is unselfish devotion. Where her happiness becomes a beautiful melody, even when the chords struck the bittersweet hymns of releasing her to the winds of freedom.

41. Nitika Khanna

The acrid taste of disaster
Heavy on my tongue
Tell me a way to attack faster ,
than words begotten to stung .

The unbearable weight of responsiblity
Heavy on my arms
Tell me a more sinful liberty ,
than actions intended to send alarms .

The vulnerability of fear
Heavy on my legs
Tell me a way to break and tear ,
Than bonds broken with as much ease as threads.

Sensitivity of grief
Heavy on my heart
Tell me a more crooked thief ,
than dreams that fell apart...

42. Sayantani Roy

FROM ASHES TO AURORA

In silken shadows, where darkness dwelled
A splash of acid, a life compelled
To rewrite fate, to reforge the soul
A phoenix rising, from charred control
Amidst the ashes, a voice whispered low
"You are not your scars, nor your woe"
A heart, once shattered, now mends with gold
A tapestry of strength, forever to unfold
With every breath, a new dawn breaks
A defiance born, from acid's snakes
The hiss of hate, the sting of pain
Transmuted into courage, an unyielding refrain
Like lotus blooms, in murky depths
You rise, untainted, in radiant breaths
Petals of resilience, unfolding slow
A testament to life's unbroken flow
Your face, a canvas, of trials and strife
Now shines, a masterpiece, of renewed life
Eyes, once dimmed, now blaze like stars
Reflecting the fire, that fuels your scars
In this crucible, of suffering and pain
You've discovered strength, an unyielding refrain
A symphony of hope, echoing through time
A phoenix rising, sublime.

43. Mehak Amir

You think you are gratuitous having no motive,
Living like a dud having no point of view,
Just born groundless like those koalas,
Squander their life by losing in obvious sleep

It's you and your mind who stops you to see the sky,
To adorn the beauty of life, but you are busy in finding the way to fly,
There is no need to find the ways which are futile for your life,
If you think so you were nothing, you are nothing, you were never alive

44. SAKTHI

THE INSANE LOVE
                                -SAKTHI

A man with magnetic eyes
She's starving to put her head on his thighs!!
He started gifting her with roses
And their love is moving in high paces!!
She started looking at him
And he started looking over a gym!!
She likes her chai hot
And he became her Chai pot!!
He started walking for her
And she clasped his hands forever!!
His ears are waiting for her words
And he started fulfilling her words!!
He started waiting for her smile
And all his pain flew away by her smile!!
He started sniffing her clothes
Then for a second his blood clots!!
Their love is growing in a chilly fog
As soon as he became her dog!!
Always he seeks for her heart mail
And finally all those a fairytale!!.....

45. Anu Rajpoot

"हम से अहम की लड़ाई में,
 कितना कुछ पीछे छूट गया।
हमको अजनबी बना, वो
 कितना आगे निकल गया।
इंतजार होता है हमें कि शायद,
 अब बोलेगा वो कुछ।
ऐसा नहीं है कि बोलता नहीं है कुछ,
 जब भी बोलता है किस्तों में बोलता है।
और हम जो बोले उसे भी,
 नाप-तौल के रखता है।
उसका कुछ सुनना अब तो जैसे,
 नामुमकिन सा हो गया।
ये जो पहले 'हम' हुआ करता था,
 ना जाने कब 'मैं' में बदल गया।
हम से अहम की लड़ाई में,
 कितना कुछ पीछे छूट गया,
हमको अजनबी बना वो कैसे आगे बढ़ गया।।

46. Soumya Kashyap

ऐसा क्या बिगाड़ा मैंने किसी का ?
हो गया ही सबसे जुदा
यू आखों में आसू, खून से लपटा बदन
क्यों है ये दुनिया मुझसे ख़फ़ा ?
अब पाओगे मुझे लपटा इन कफ़न
क्या थी मेरी ख़ता?

थक गया ? या तो हार गया ?
पूछता मुझसे ख़ुदा
क्यों था तू इतना बेताब आने को यहाँ ?

आये ख़ुदा !
यू हाथों ने ना किया आज तक किसी का क़तल
ख़ुद को मार डाला
अब नहीं पूछता कोई मेरी अलामत
ना आता कोई मेरी दस्तकों पर पूछने मेरी हालत
ख़फ़ा है दुनिया मेरीस और मैं आपसे
इंज़ाम है आप पर, कोई पेश करो यह अदालत
तनहाइयों की किताब लिखी है मैंने
पर फ़रियाद करूँ भी तो किससे?
आये ख़ुदा !
लोगो ने रखी है मेरी कमियों की किताब
या कोई खड़ा उधार माँगने मेरे जनाज़े पे पास

आये ख़ुदा !
मिटा दो मेरा वजूद
बह गया मेरा ग़ुरूर
दिख गई हक़ीक़त
बना दिया दुनिया ने मुझे महरूम

47. Aniruddh Sharma

In the silent hours of the night,
I find light in her memory,
As she dances through my dreams,
A vision of beauty and grace.

Her laughter echoes in my mind,
A melody that soothes my soul,
Her touch lingers on my skin,
A gentle caress that lulls me to peace.

I reach out for her in the darkness,
But she slips away like a ghost,
Leaving only the memory of her smile,
A fleeting moment of happiness.

Yet in my dreams, she remains,
A beacon of light in the shadows,
Guiding me through the night,
Until morning breaks and she fades away.

48. Disha Darshan Shah

नाम ::: मेरी आशिकी तुम से ही.......

वैसे गुलाब प्यार ओर दोस्ती का प्रतीक होता है,गुलाब के रंग तो बहुत सारे है जैसे पीला दोस्ती का तो केसरी पक्की दोस्ती का,ओर सफेद सारे गिले शिकवे मिटाकर वापस से एक अच्छे सच्चे दोस्त बनने की शुरुआत का,ओर सबसे आखरी है लाल गुलाब !!!!! लाल गुलाब का मतलब है प्यार !!!!!.........

जब हम किसी से बहुत प्यार करते है और उसको एक लाल गुलाब देकर हम बिना कुछ कहें अपने प्यार का इज़हार कर देते हैं।।।वैसे प्यार एक खुबसूरत ओर प्यारा अह्सास होता है।वैसे हम प्यार को देख तो नहीं सकते पर महसूस जरुर कर सकतें हैं।प्यार में शब्दो की नहीं एक अह्सास की जरूरत है।

लोग कहते हैं ना......प्यार में इंसान बदल जाता है अच्छे से बुरे बन जाते हैं ओर बुरे अच्छे बन जाते हैं।वैसे प्यार करना ओर प्यार करने वाले का दिल तोडना जितना आसान है उतना ही अपने प्यार को अच्छी तरह से निभाना मुश्किल है प्यार निभाने के लिए अंडर-स्टेंडिंग और कम्युनिकेशन बहुत जरुरी है।।।।।।।।

मेरी इस कहानी में भी कुछ एसा ही हुआ हैं। दो लोग एक दुसरे को प्यार तो करतें हैं पर एक गलत फैमी के कारण ओर किसी के गलत इरादे के कारण वे लोग अलग हो जाते है पर उनका प्यार सच्चा होने की वजह से वे एक ना एक दिन एक हो ही जाते है।।।।"प्यार में दुरी जरुर आ जाती है पर प्यार कभी भी अधुरा नहीं रहता।वह समय और नियती के साथ एक हो ही जाता हैं।"

एक बड़े घर का लड़का अभिनव खुराना देखनें में जितना हैंडसम ओर चार्मिंग उतना ही स्वभाव से शांत ओर कम मिलनसार वैसे अभिनव के पापा मानव खुराना दिल्ली के सबसे बड़ा बिज़नेस थें।अभिनव खुराना का परिवार दिल्ली के परिवारों मैसे एक परिवार था। अभिनव अपनी मां से बहुत प्यार करता था,उसकी मां की मौत के बाद वह बहुत ही अकेला महसूस करने लगा था।मां के जाने के बाद दादी ही एक ऐसी इंसान थी जिसके वह सबसे करीब था। पर एक दिन दादी की भी मौत हो गई इसलिए वह ओर भी शांत ओर उदास हो गया।अभिनव कहीं ना कहीं यही सोच रहा था की वह जिससे भी प्यार करता है वह उससे छोड़कर चला जाता है,इसलिए वह सबसे अलग ही रहने लगा था। अभिनव अपने पापा की रिस्पेक्ट करता था ओर प्यार भी करता था पर वह अपना प्यार जताता नहीं था और काम सिखने के लिए ऑफिस में भी आता था,पर उन दोनों के बीच इतनी कम्युनिकेशन नहीं होती थी पर अभिनव की लाइफ में उसका एक दोस्त था विनय कपूर। जब भी अभिनव उदास होता था तब वह अपने दोस्त के साथ ड्रिंक करके सारी दिल की बात बताता था।

वैसे अभिनव पढ़ाई मे एवरेज था।दुसरी तरफ संजना गुप्ता एक मिडल क्लास लडकी।दिखने में जितनी सिंपल उतनी ही खूबसूरत ओर अट्रैक्टीव।वैसे संजना बहुत ही चंचल ओर मस्ती बाज़ लड़की थीं और उसका स्वभाव मिलनसार था।वैसे संजना के पिताजी की मौत के बाद सारा घर का भार उसके ओर उसकी मां शालिनी गुप्ता के उपर आ गया था,पर इतनी मुश्किलों के बाद भी संजना खुश मिज़ाज में अपनी लाइफ जीती थी।वह हमेशा सोचती थीं की लाइफ में मुश्किलो की कमी नहीं है पर उसके बीच अपना जीवन रुकता नही है तो हम जीना क्यों छोड़ें।वैसे संजना पढ़ाई मे बहुत ही होशियार थी और उसकी एक ही बेस्ट फ्रेंड थी छाया शर्मा।वैसे छाया का परिवार संजना के परिवार से काफी अच्छा था।संजना अपनी मां की मदद करने लिए छोटा मोटा काम भी करती थी ओर साथ मे पढ़ाई भी। एक दिन संजना को १२ के बोर्ड में पुरे दिल्ली बहुत ही अच्छा स्कोर किया था, इसलिए उसे ठाकुर कोलेज में स्कॉलरशिप मिली थी। जहां पर बड़े बड़े घर परिवार के लोग एडमीशन लेते थें।वैसे अभिनव ने भी यहा एडमीशन लिया था।उन दोनों ने कॉमर्स लिया था।ओर इतेफाक से उन दोनों का क्लास रूम ऐक ही था।आज उन दोनों के कोलेज का पहला दिन था।जब छाया ओर संजना पहली बार कॉलेज को बाहर से देखा तो वे लोग देखते ही रह गए। बाद में वे लोग कॉलेज के अंदर गए ओर वे लोग क्लास के अंदर जाने वाले होते है तब अचानक संजना का पैर मुड़ता है गलती से उसी समय अभिनव जो उसके पीछे खड़ा हुआ था उसने संजना को गिरने से बचा लेता है और।तब ही पहली बार संजना ओर अभिनव मिले फीर उनकी आंखे एक दुसरे से टकराई और वे लोग थोडी देर एक दुसरे को ऐसे ही देखते रहे जब संजना को छाया ने ओर अभिनव को विनय ने बुलाया तब वे लोग होश मे आए और अभिनव ने संजना को खड़े करके छोड़ दिया ओर बिना कुछ कहें वहा से चला गया और संजना बस उसको देखती ही रह गई। उसके बाद संजना छाया को बोली," कितना अजीब इन्सान था,थैंक्यू बोलने भी नही दिया"।तब छाया एक्साइटेड होकर बोली," पता है यह इंसान कोन है ? यह और कोई ओर नही खुराना कंपनी के मालिक का एक लौता बेटा है। यह सुनकर संजना नोर्मल पर एटीट्यूड दिखाते हुए बोली, "तो हमे क्या करना वह किसी का बेटा हो हमे तो बस अपनी पढ़ाई पर ध्यान देना चाहिए।"यह सब बात करते करते वे लोग क्लास के अंदर आ जाते है,क्लास के अंदर आने के बाद संजना अभिनव को एक नजर देखतीं है तब छाया बोलती है अभी तु उस तरफ क्यों देख रही है?तब संजना कहती है की,"मै उसे इस लिए देख रही थी क्योंकि मुझे बस उसको थैंक्यू कहना था, पर वह तो मेरी तरफ देख कर मुह घुमा दिया, "सच मे बहुत ही अकडु है यह तो "। तब छाया कहती है,"हैंडसम लडके ऐसे ही होते है"। तब संजना बोली," मैं एक बार उसको थैंक्स तो पक्का कहुंगी !! नही तो मुझे निंद नही आएंगी"। तब छाया बोली,"तेरी मर्जी पर फिलहाल तो सर आए तो थोडी पढ़ाई कर लेते है"? संजना बोली ,"हा!!!!"

जब लेक्चर खत्म हुआ तब संजना अभिनव के पास गई ओर उसको थैंक्स कहने के लिए तब अभिनव पहले तो उसको देखा उसके बाद इस ओके!!!! कहकर वहां से चला गया तब संजना को उसके व्यवहार से गुस्सा आया ओर वह बोली की कितना रुड इंसान है तब पीछे से विनय कहता है, अभिनव रुड नहीं है पर वह बहुत कम बात करता है।बाय द वे, मैं विनय हु ओर आप?(ओर यह कहकर विनय अपना हाथ आगे बढाता है) ,(तब संजना हाथ मिलाकर)मैं संजना!!

विनय:नए हो क्या?
संजना:नही
(छाया भाग कर आती है ,ओर संजना से कहती है)
छाया:क्या यार तु मुझे छोड़कर आ गई।
(संजना विनय को देखकर कहती है)
संजना:यह मैरी दोस्त छाया।
विनय (हाथ मिलाकर):हाई!! नाइस टु मीट यू।
संजना:वैसे वह मतलब,,,, अभिनव कम बात क्यों करता है?
विनय(हस्ते हुए):वह पहले से ऐसा है।
संजना:ओहो!!!!
विनय (सोचते हुए और बात को बदलते हुए):तुम लोगों को मैंने पहले यहां नहीं देखा?
संजना:हम लोग नए है इधर इसलिए।
छाया:वैसे आप अभिनव के पक्के वालें दोस्त हों?
विनय:हा!!! क्यों,पुछ रही हों?
छाया:बस ऐसे ही।
विनय(संजना को देखकर):तुम सिरीयसली बहुत ही ज्यादा सुंदर हो।
संजना(हस्ते हुए):प्लीज यह कहकर मेरे साथ फल्ट करना चालु मत कर देना?
विनय (बात को क्लीयर करके): नहीं.......नहीं......! मैं तो बस !! मुझे जो लगा वह मैने कह दिया।वैसे मेरा कोई ओर इरादा नहीं है।
संजना (हस्ते हुए):तुम टेंशन मत लो मै मज़ाक कर रही थी।
विनय(खुशी के मारे हाथ आगे करके):फ्रेंड्स?
संजना(खुशी के मारे हाथ मिलाकर):फ्रेंड्स। ।।।
छाया(एक्साइटेड होकर हाथ आगे करके):मै भी फ्रेंड्स?
विनय (हाथ मिलाकर ओर हंसकर):हा!!!!!

ऐसे ही वे लोग बात करते करते वहां से चलें गए। दूसरे दिन से अभिनव, विनय और संजना,छाया वे लोग साथ मे बैठ ने लगे और साथ मे लेक्चर मे भी बैठ ने लगे पर संजना को कहीं ना कहीं अभिनव का समझ में नहीं आता था,वे लोग साथ बैठते थे विनय मस्ती करता था पर अभिनव बस शांत ही बैठा हुआ रहता था।संजना को अभिनव के बारे मे जान ने की एक कयुरीयोसीटी होने लगी थी।इसलिए वह अभिनव को ओबझव करने लगीं और दुसरी तरफ छाया अभिनव के हैंडसम चहरे और उसके एटीट्यूड के कारण उस पर फिदा होने लगी थीं और छाया अभिनव को प्यार करने लगी थीं। देखते ही देखते एक महीना खत्म हुआ ओर वे चारो बहुत ही अच्छे वाले दोस्त बन गए। ओर बाद में उन लोगों को एक ग्रुप प्रोजेक्ट मिला था तो उस प्रोजेक्ट पर काम करते करते संजना ओर अभिनव विनय ओर छाया ओर भी ज़्यादा समय बिताने लगे प्रोजेक्ट के दौरान अभिनव इनडायरेकटली संजना की मदद करता था।पर कहीं ना कहीं संजना जानती थीं उसकी मदद ओर कोई नहीं अभिनव करता था,पर वह जताता नही था !!!!उसके यह अंदाज से संजना उसकी तरफ थोडी थोडी अट्रैक्ट हो रही थी।ओर छाया ने महसूस किया की संजना कहीं ना कहीं अभिनव के तरफ अट्रैक्ट हो रही है,पहले तो उसको थोडा गुस्सा आया की वह अभिनव के कैसे करीब जा सकती है?क्योंकि मैं अभिनव से प्यार करती हु।थोडे समय के बाद अपने गुस्से को शांत करके छाया ने सोचा की वह डायरेक्ट संजना से पुछले इसलिए वह संजना के पास जाकर उसको घुमा-फिराकर पूछती है

छाया:क्या बात है आज कल तुम कुछ ज्यादा अभिनव के करीब जा रही हो,ओर उसको घूरती रहती हैं?प्यार हो गया है क्या?

संजना(कॉन्फिडेंस के साथ):नही!!! मैं थोडी ना पागल हुं की, मै ऐसे इंसान को प्यार करुंगी जो सिर्फ शांत रहना पसंद है। मेरी चोइस इतनी भी बुरी नहीं है !!!,,, मैं इत्तेफ़ाक से उसको देखती हुं।।।"

यह सब सुनकर छाया के दिल को सुकून मिला। एक दिन संजना उदास होकर कोलेज के कैंटीन मे बैठीं थी,तब विनय ने संजना को उदास होकर बैठें हुए देखा तो उसे रहा नही गया ओर वह संजना के पास जाकर बैठ गया।

विनय:कुछ हुआ है क्या?

संजना(उदास होकर):हा!! अभी बहुत टेंशन है?

विनय (टेंशन मे):क्या हुआ?

संजना(गंभीर होकर):मुझे जोब करना है, मेने दो जगह पर एप्लीकेशन डाला था जोब के लिए पर उनका अब तक कोई जवाब नही आया है और मुझे अपनी मां की मदद करनी है पर दिल्ली शहर मे काम मिलना कितना मुश्किल है?।।।।।। तो मैं सोच रही थी की मुझे जोब कहां मिलेंगी?

विनय (संजना को समझाते):तुम टेंशन मत लो तुम्हे जोब मिल जाएं गी। मैं कुछ करता हु।।

संजना(खुश होकर):क्या तुम मेरी मदद करोंगे?

विनय:हा!!!! अभी उदास होकर मत बैठो चलों घर वैसे लेट हो गया है।यह कहकर वे लोग वहां से चले जाते हैं

पर इत्तेफाक से यह सारी बात अभिनव सुन लेता है,पहले थोडी देर सोचने के बाद रात को अभिनव विनय को कोल करता है

अभिनव: हाई क्या कर रहा है?
विनय(सोते सोते):तु इस वक्त यह पूछने के लिए कोल किया है?
अभिनव कुछ सेकंड के लिए चुप रहा उसके बाद,
अभिनव:मैने आज तेरी ओर संजना की सारी बात सूनी।
विनय(कन्फ्यूज हो कर):कोन सी बात?
अभिनव:जो तु ओर संजना बात कर रहे थे जोब को लेकर।
विनय: हां हां !!!तो?
अभिनव:मेरे कंपनी मे एक फिमैल इम्प्लोइ की जरूरत है,और संजना उस काम के लिए बडी़या रहेंगी तो कल उसको मेरे ऑफिस भेज देना मै अभी एच आर से बात करके रखता हु।
विनय (कन्फ्यूजन मे): तु उसकी मदद क्यों करना चाहता है? प्यार व्यार हों गया हैं उससे?
अभिनव (गुस्से मे): तुझे जो काम करने को बोला है वो कर ओके।
विनय:हा बाबा,मै कह दुंगा।"

दुसरे दिन सुबह विनय संजना को कोल करता है और कहता है की तुम्हे जोब करनी है ना?तो आज इंटरव्यू के लिए अभिनव के कंपनी मे चली जाओ तुम्हे जोब मिल जाएंगी।यह सुनकर संजना विनय को थैंक्यू कहतीं है और तैयार हो कर अभिनव के ऑफिस चलीं जाती है और वह सिलेक्ट भी हो जाती है।दुसरे दिन संजना काम पर चलीं जाती है। तो काम पर उसको अभिनव दिखता है तो वह खुशी के मारे एक्साइटेड होकर उसको हाय!! कहकर कहती है, "मैं तुम्हारे साथ इस फर्म में करने वाली हु,तो आज से हम साथ मे काम करेंगे,पर अभिनव उसको देखता है ओर वहां से बिना कुछ कहें चला जाता है।उसका ऐसा व्यवहार देखकर संजना को बहुत गुस्सा आता है और वहां से जाकर अपने डेस्क मे बैठ जाती है,ओर अपना काम संभाल ने लगती है पर अपने केबिन के पीछे से अभिनव उसको देखता है और जब संजना को पता चला की इस फर्म के दुसरे फ्लोर पर एक लाइब्रेरी है ,तो संजना को कभी भी समय मिलता था तब वह कुछ ना कुछ पढ़ने के लिए लाइब्रेरी जाती थीं क्योकि उसको किताबे पढ़ना बहुत पसंद था और अभिनव को भी किताब पढ़ना बहुत पसंद था तो वह भी जाता था।तब संजना कोशिश करती थी अभिनव से बात करने की पर अभिनव सिर्फ हां ना ओर ओके बस यही कहता था।

देखते ही देखते संजना को उस फर्म में काम करते करते एक महीना हो गया और संजना के मस्ती ओर चुलबुले स्वभाव के कारण अभिनव भी थोडा खुश रहने लगा था ओर जो इंसान हमेशा अपने चहरे पर गंभीर ओर सिरीयस एक्सप्रेशन रखने वाले पर मुस्कान आने लगीं थी।अभिनव कोलेज ओर ऑफिस मे ज्यादातर संजना के साथ समय बिताने लगा था।जब यह सब छाया देखतीं थीं तब उसको संजना पर बहुत गुस्सा ओर जलन आता था।एक दिन ऑफिस मे एक आदमी को पैसें की बहुत जरूरत आन पडी थी तब अभिनव ने बीना कुछ सोचे उसकी मदद कर दी।यह बात संजना के दिल को छु गई। जब संजना अपने ऑफिस का काम कर रही होती है तब उसका फोन बजता है तब वह नाम देखती है तो विनय का नाम देखकर वह फोन उठा लेती है।

विनय:क्या यार आज कल तुम बहुत बिज़ी हो गई है?दोस्तो के लिए तो समय ही नही है?
संजना:ऐसा नही है यार!!बस काम ज्यादा होता है इसलिए।
विनय:वैसे अभिनव तुम्हारा ख्याल रखता है? वहां पे ?सोरी!!!!मैने गलत सवाल पूछा तुमसे?
संजना(कन्फ्यूजन मे):मतलब?
विनय:जो इन्सान ने तुम्हे जोब दिलवाई है वो तो तुम्हार ख्याल तो रखेगा ना।
संजना(चौक ते हुए चिल्लाकर):क्या?
विनय: हा उस समय अभिनव ने हमारी सारी बाते सुन ली थी, ओर उसने ही मुझे कहा था की तुम्हे यहा इंटरव्यू के लिए भेजु इसके लिए मैंने तुम्हें यहां भेजा था।
संजना(बहाना करके):विनय मुझे कुछ काम आ गया है तो मै तुमसे बाद मे बात करती हु। यह कहकर उसने फोन रख दिया।

उसके फोन रखने बाद ओर यह न्युज मिलने के बाद अभिनव ने ही उसकी मदद की थी।वह जान ने के बाद उसके दिल मे एक अलग ही अह्सास अभिनव के लिए होने लगा और अभिनव के लिए उसकी इज्जत और भी बड गई।जब अभिनव ओर संजना लाइब्रेरी में होते है और दोनो का बुक पढ़ना हो जाता है तब अभिनव उसको अपनी बुक थमाकर कहता हैं की प्लीज तुम मैरी बुक रख दो गी।मुझे कुछ काम याद आ गया है यह कहकर अभिनव वहा से चला जाता है।देखते ही देखते सावन का महीना आ जाता है ओर उस समय संजना उपवास करती थी पर एक दिन वह खाने पीने की कमी के कारण वह बेहोश हो कर गिरने वाली होती है तब अभिनव उसको पकड़कर अपनी बाहो मे भरता है उसी समय छाया संजना को फल ओर कुछ उपवास के नास्ते के बहानें और अभिनव को मिलने के बहाने आती है तब छाया यह नज़ारा देखकर चौंक जाती है जब अभिनव संजना की बहुत परवाह करते देख छाया को बहुत दुख होता है और वह किसी को बीना बताएं वहां से चली जाती है।जब अभिनव उसको होश मे लाकर उसको थोड़ा ज़बरदस्ती खिलाने की कोशिश करता है तब संजना ना कहकर कहती है की आज मेरा उपवास है तो मैं नहीं खा सकतीं तब अभिनव उसको चिल्लाकर थोडा खाना खिला देता है।अभिनव के एसे व्यवहार से संजना उसको पंसद करने लगती है।उसके बाद वे लोग काम की वजह से या फिर खाने की वजह से ज्यादातर समय बीता ने लगे और संजना को देखते ही देखते अभिनव से प्यार हो जाता है।संजना ओर अभिनव को इतने करीब आते देख छाया को बहुत बुरा लगता है ओर वह हद से ज्यादा जलन के मारे वह संजना से नफरत करने लगती है और सोचती है की, मै उन दोनों को एक बिल्कुल नही होने दुंगी तब छाया एक प्लान बनाती है और उन दोनो के बीच ग़लत फहमी करने की सोचती है।वह अपने आप से कहती है की तूने मेरे से अभिनव को छीना है ना तो मैं अभिनव को तेरा भी नही होने दुंगी।।दुसरे दिन जब अभिनव कोलेज पहुंचता है तब संजना विनय के साथ मस्ती कर रही होती है तब अभिनव संजना को विनय से मस्ती करते देख मुस्कुरा रहा होता है तब छाया अभिनव के पास आती है और कहती है की, "विनय ओर संजना कितने क्यूट लग रहे है ना साथ में !!!!!ओर उनकी जोडी भी बहुत क्यूट हैं ना??"

जब जोड़ी के बारे मे अभिनव ने सुना तो वह चौंक गया ओर थोडे समय पहले जो मुस्कान थी वह गायब हो गई।अभिनव ने छाया से पूछा जोड़ी मतलब??तब छाया मासूम चहेरा बनाकर कहतीं है की क्या तुम्हे नहीं पता संजना विनय को पंसद करती है ?ओर विनय भी।बस इकरार करना बाकी है।जब यह सब अभिनव ने सुना तों वह गुस्से ओर उदास होकर चला गया और अभिनव को एसे जाते देख छाया एक शातिर हंसी हस्ती है और कहती है की ,"प्यार मे ग़लत फ़हमी की हल्की दीवार तो खडी कर दी है",बस अभी एक काम ओर बाकी है उसके बाद पुरी दिवार खडी कर दुंगी उन दोनों के बीच में।यह कहकर वह अपने दुसरे प्लान में लग जाती है।जब अभिनव उदास ओर गुस्सा होकर बैठा हुआ रहता है तब छाया उसके पास जाती है ओर उसको पूछतीं है की कुछ हुआ है क्या?तब अभिनव कहता हैं की मुझे बस थोडी देर अकेला रहने दो जब छाया वहा से जाने वाली होती है तब वह देखतीं है की संजना अभिनव को मिलने आ रही होती है तब वह अभिनव के सामने आकर नाटक करके कहती है की अभिनव देखो ना मेरी आंख मे कुछ चला गया है ।तब अभिनव देखता है छाया को बहुत दर्द हो रहा तो वह खड़ा होकर उसकी मदद कर रहा होता है।तब पीछे से संजना को लगता है,अभिनव ओर छाया किस कर रहे है!!यह नजारा देख कर संजना चौंक कर ओर उदास होकर वहां से भाग जाती है।यह देखकर छाया के चहरे पर फिर से शातिर मुस्कान आ जाती है। पहले तो अभिनव से रहा नही गया पर वह रात का इन्तज़ार कर रहा था क्योंकि वे लोग रोज रात को क्लब में जाते थे इसलिए जब रात को अभिनव ने और विनय क्लब में मिले जहां वे लोग रोज मिलते हैं रोज की तरह बेट मिनटन खेलने के बाद वे लोग शांती से बैठे तब अभिनव ने बात चालु की काम को लेकर जब काम की बात खत्म हुईं तब अभिनव ने बातों ही बातों में पूछा की कोई लडकी पंसद आई है क्या?तब विनय ने कहां अचानक यह सवाल क्यो? नहीं मेंने देखा की आज कल तु संजना के बहुत करीब आ रहा है तो मुझे महसूस हुआ इस के लिए पूछा ?ऐसा है तो बता दे ?दोस्त से क्या छुपाना ?तब वह शरमाते बता देता है की वह संजना को पंसद करता है ओर कहता हैं की मुझे कहीं ना कहीं यह लग रहा है की वह भी मुझे पंसद करती है।यह सुनकर पहले तो अभिनव चुप हो गया। वह अपनी उदासी किसी को बतानी नहीं थी इसीलिए उसके बाद वह कुछ काम का बहाना करके निकल गया। दुसरी तरफ संजना ने छाया से पूछा की वह ओर अभिनव एक रिलेशनशिप में है?तब छाया जहरीली मुस्कान के साथ हा कहकर कहती है की मुझे तेरे को यह पहले बताना था पर नहीं बता पाई क्योंकि तु बहुत व्यस्त थी,अपने काम मे।संजना मे ओर कुछ ओर सुनने की हिम्मत नहीं थीं तो इसलिए वह भी कुछ बहाना करके वहा से निकल गईं।उसको उदास जाकर देख छाया बहुत ही खुश हो रही थी।बात करने के बाद संजना को बहुत ही रोना आ रहा था तो वह रो रहीं थी। दुसरी तरफ अभिनव अपने आप को कमरे मे बंध करके अपनी मां की फोटो को गले लगाकार वह भी रो रहा था।उस दिन के बाद वे लोग एक दुसरे को अवॉइड करने लगे पर संजना को अभिनव की बहुत याद आ रही थी इसलिए वह लाइब्रेरी चली गई। जब वह लाइब्रेरी मे पहुंची तब उसकी नजर उस बुक पर गई जो लास्ट टाइम अभिनव ने पढा था जब संजना उस बुक निकाल रही थी तब उसके हाथ से ग़लती से वह बुक गिर जाती है।जब वह बुक उठाने जाती है तो उस बुक मेसे एक गुलाब ओर एक लेटर निकलता है वह यह सब देखकर वह चौंक जाती है ।ओर अच्छे से देखने के बाद उसको पता चलता है की वह लेटर किसी ओर ने नही बल्कि खुद अभिनव ने लिखा था उसके लिए।

तुम्हे यही लगता होगा ना!!! मै यह चिट्ठी क्यों लिख रहां हुं बहुत हिम्मत के बाद सोचा की जो मै तुम्हारे लिए महसूस करता हु वह मै तुम्हे बता दु की ,"मै तुमसे प्यार करता हु❤❤❤" वो भी उस समय से जब से मै तुम्हे पहली बार देखा पता नही तुम मे ऐसा क्या था की तुम्हे देखते ही मुझे तुमसे प्यार हो गया❤❤❤।ओर तुम्हारा मासुम चेहरा ओर तुम्हारी प्यारी आंखो को देखकर मै तुम पे फिदा हो गया।और तुम्हारी बचपने जैसी हरकत से मैं तुम्हारी तरफ कब अट्रैक्ट होने लगा मुझे पता ही नहीं चला□□□।, मैं पहले से ही तुमसे अच्छे से बात नही करता था क्योंकि मुझे डर लगता था तुम भी मुझे अपनी मां ओर दादी की तरह छोड़कर चली जाओ गी,पर मुझे आज महसूस हुआ की मै तुम्हारे बिना नही रह पाउंगा फिर भी तुम्हे सबके सामने बोलने की हिम्मत नही हो रही थी इसलिए मै यह खत लिखकर ओर तुम्हारा मनपसंद लाल गुलाब यह किताब के बीच मे रख रहा हु।जो तुम्हे मेरा प्यार कबुल हो तो मुझे सबके साम ने गले लगा देना।ओर तुम्हे मेरा प्यार मंजूर ना हो तो मेरे पास आ कर चलीं जाना मै समझ जाउंगा की तुम मुझसे प्यार नहीं करतीं।जो भी तुम्हारा फैसला हो तो मै उसकी इज्जत करुंगा। यह खत पढ़ने के बाद संजना पुरी तरह से चौंक जाती है,फिर वह बिना कुछ सोचे अभिनव के पास चली जाती है।जब संजना उसके केबिन मे जाकर अभिनव को गले लगा कर पूछती है की तुमने सच क्यो छिपाया?अभिनव संजना के ऐसे लगे मिलने से पहले तो चौंक जाता है और संजना को खुद से अलग करके पूछता है क्या छिपाया मैंने?तब संजना वह खत दिखाती है।वह खत देखकर अभिनव चौंक कर पूछता है की, तुमने अभी यह पढ़ा मैंने यह लेटर तुम्हे एक हफ्ते पहले लिखा था पर तुम बुक रखकर वापस आ कर चली गई तब मुझे लगा की तुम्हे मैं पंसद नही हू ।तब संजना कहती है की मैंने उस किताब को बस ऐसे ही रख दिया था इसलिए मुझे पता नहीं था।तब अभिनव कहता है की, हा!!! तुम ध्यान क्यों दोगी, क्योंकि तुम तो विनय से प्यार करती हो।जब संजना ने यह सुना तो वह चौंक कर बोली तुम्हे किसने बताया की मै विनय से प्यार करती हु,तब अभिनव छाया का नाम लेकर कहता है की उसने बताया।यह सुनकर संजना ओर भी ज्यादा चौंक जाती है ओर अपने आप से बात कहकर कहती है की छाया ने ऐसा क्यों कहां?जब अभिनव ने सुना यह तब अभिनव कहता है की क्योंकि तुम विनय से प्यार करती हो इसलिए तब संजना चिल्लाकर कहती है अभिनव से मै विनय से नही तुमसे प्यार करती हु!@!@@@ तो प्लीज तुम बार बार यह कहना छोड़ दो की मै विनय से प्यार करती हु। में तुम्हे उस दिन अपने प्यार का इजहार करने आई थी पर तुम खुद छाया को किस कर रहे थे,तो मैं वहां से उदास होकर चली गई।तुम भी छाया के साथ रिलेशनशिप मे हो ? मैंने तुम्हे कुछ कहा?? तुम मेरे को क्या बोल रहे हो!!!!!! अभिनव यह सुनकर हक्का बक्का हो जाता है, बाद मे वह बात को क्लियर करके कहता है मैं कभी भी किसी के साथ रिलेशनशिप में नहीं गया क्योंकि मैं भी तुमसे प्यार करता हु वो भी पहले से!!!!! ।उस दिन छाया की आंख मे कुछ चला गया था इसलिए मै सिर्फ उसकी मदद कर रहा था बस।।पर रिलेशनशिप की बात की किसने?तब संजना कहती है की मुझे छाया ने बताया। ऐसे ही बातों ही बातों में वे लोग अपने प्यार का इज़हार कर देते है और उनको पता ही नही चलता। जब उन लोगो का जगड ना बंद होता है ओर शांत होते है तब उन दोनों को रियलाइज होता है कुछ मिनट पहले उन लोगों ने अपने प्यार का इजहार किया है।तब संजना तो शरमा जाती है पर अभिनव उसको बाहों में भरकर किस कर लेता

है।थोडे समय के बाद संजना अभिनव को कहती है की मुझे एकबार छाया से बात करनी है क्योंकि जो हमारे बीच मे ग़लत फहमी हुई है वह सब छाया के कारण हुई है। तब अभिनव उसको बाहों में भरकर ओर थोडी देर सोच कर कहता है की, कल तुम बात कर लेना अभी देर हो गई है, तब संजना हा मे सिर हिला कर ,,हा कहती है।

दूसरे दिन वह छाया से मिलने कोलेज जाती है।ओर वह छाया कैन्टीन मे मिलती है तब संजना ने नो हाई ओर हेलो तुरंत ही उसके मुह पर थप्पड मार कर कहां की तुमने जो यह सब किया है ना बहुत ही ज्यादा गलत किया है पहले तो छाया को समझ नहीं आ रहा होता की संजना क्या बात कर रही है पर संजना उसे सारी बात बता देती है और पूछती है की यह सब क्यो किया? तब छाया गुस्से मे आकर ओर उसको धक्का दे कर बोला यह सब मैंने इसलिए किया क्योंकि मैं तुमसे नफरत करती हु।।। क्योंकि तुमने मुझसे मेरा प्यार छीना है ।तो मै तुम्हे मेरे प्यार के साथ कैसे रहनें दु।यह सब सुनकर संजना चौंक कर पूछती है तुम्हारा प्यार?तब छाया कहती है की अभिनव मेरा प्यार था ,पर तुमने क्या जादु किया उस पर की वह तुमसे प्यार करने लगा।ओर उसने मेरी तरफ देखना भी छोड़ दिया।जब मेरा प्यार सफल नहीं हुआ तो मै तुम्हारा प्यार कैसे सफल होने दु और मै तुम दोनों को एक साथ नहीं देख सकतीं थी इसीलिए मैंने यह सब किया।जब पीछे से अभिनव ने यह सब सुना तब वह बोला की मैं पहले से ही संजना को प्यार करता था।।पहले से तुम मैरी अच्छी दोस्त थी। पर यह यह सब जो तुम ने जो किया है ना, इसके बाद तुम मैरी दोस्त भी नहीं रही।यह सब सुनकर छाया अंदर से टुट जाती हैं ओर अभिनव से कहती है, मैने यह सब तुम्हारे लिए किया ओर तुम इस मामुली लडकी के कारण मुझे ठुकरा रहे हो ?तब अभिनव गुस्से मे आकर बोला यह मामुली लडकी नहीं है ।।यह मेरी मंगेतर है।।।। तो जबान संभालकर!!!! ओर अभिनव छाया को घमकी देकर कहता आज के बाद जो तुमने मैरी मंगेतर को हाथ लगाया या फिर हानी पहुंचाई तो मै तुम्हे नही छोडूंगा।संजना यह सब देखकर बहुत ही इमोशनल हो जाती है,ओर उसको खुश हो कर देखती है,यह कहकर अभिनव संजना का हाथ पकडकर वहा से चला जाता है।ओर छाया बस उदास होकर उन दोनो जाते हुए देखती है।कुछ दिन बाद अभिनव संजना को अच्छे से केंडल लाईट डिनर पे लेकर जाते उसको रिंग पहना कर प्रपोज कर देता है।।।।।।।।

49. Disha Shah

कायरा की कहानी: नारी शक्ति और आत्मरक्षा

कायरा बचपन से ही एक खुशमिजाज और नटखट बच्ची थी। लेकिन जब वह केवल 12 साल की थी, तब एक घटना ने उसकी जिंदगी को पूरी तरह बदल दिया। एक दिन स्कूल से लौटते समय, उसके साथ मोलेस्टेशन की घटना हुई। उस पल ने कायरा की मासूमियत को तोड़ दिया और उसके भीतर एक गहरी चोट छोड़ दी। वह डर और सदमे में थी, और धीरे-धीरे वह अपने अंदर ही घुटने लगी। कायरा ने अपनी जिंदगी को सीमित कर लिया था, वह खुल कर हंसना और अपनी जिंदगी को जीना भूल चुकी थी। उस दर्दनाक घटना का असर इतना गहरा था कि वह समाज से कटने लगी। उसके आत्मविश्वास में भारी गिरावट आई और उसे हर व्यक्ति से डर लगने लगा।

कायरा के माता-पिता उसकी हालत से बहुत चिंतित थे, खासकर उसके पिता। उन्होंने उसे कई काउंसलिंग सत्रों में भेजा, पर कुछ खास असर नहीं हुआ। कायरा के पिता, अर्जुन शर्मा, हमेशा चाहते थे कि उनकी बेटी आत्मनिर्भर और निडर बने। लेकिन वे उसकी हालत देखकर बहुत ही चिंतित थे। कायरा पढ़ाई में भी पहले जैसी नहीं रही, वह खुद को हमेशा अकेला और असहाय महसूस करती थी।

एक दिन, कायरा के पिता ने एक नए बॉक्सिंग कोच, समीर वर्मा, से मुलाकात की। समीर एक युवा, सफल बॉक्सर थे और उन्होंने कई पुरस्कार भी जीते थे। कायरा के पिता ने उनसे कायरा की मदद करने का अनुरोध किया। उन्होंने कहा, "मेरी बेटी कायरा अपने अंदर के डर से जूझ रही है। वह उस भयावह घटना के बाद से खुलकर नहीं जी पा रही है। क्या आप उसकी मदद कर सकते हैं?"

समीर वर्मा ने कायरा से मिलने का निर्णय लिया। जब वे पहली बार कायरा से मिले, तो उन्होंने देखा कि उसकी आँखों में गहरे दर्द और निराशा के बादल छाए हुए थे। लेकिन समीर को यह भी महसूस हुआ कि उसके भीतर एक आग छिपी हुई है, एक शक्ति जो सही दिशा में जाने पर कायरा को अपने डर से उबार सकती है।

समीर ने कायरा को धीरे-धीरे समझाने की कोशिश की। उन्होंने कहा, "कायरा, तुम्हारा डर तुम्हें रोक रहा है। पर एक बात याद रखो, यह दुनिया कभी भी पूरी तरह से सुरक्षित नहीं हो सकती, पर तुम खुद को इतना मजबूत बना सकती हो कि कोई तुम्हारे साथ गलत न कर सके। तुम सिर्फ अपने लिए नहीं, बल्कि हर उस लड़की के लिए लड़ सकती हो जो आज भी डर के साये में जी रही है। तुम्हें अपनी नारी शक्ति को पहचानना होगा।"

कायरा ने पहले समीर की बातों को अनसुना कर दिया। वह किसी से भी नज़दीकी संबंध बनाने से डरती थी, खासकर अजनबियों से। लेकिन समीर हार मानने वालों में से नहीं थे। वे धीरे-धीरे कायरा के करीब आने लगे, उसे छोटे-छोटे कदमों से उसकी आत्मरक्षा सिखाने लगे।

समीर ने कायरा को सेल्फ डिफेंस की ट्रेनिंग देने का फैसला किया। उन्होंने उसे आत्मरक्षा के बेसिक तकनीकें सिखानी शुरू कीं, जैसे कि किसी हमले के समय खुद को कैसे बचाया जाए, कैसे किसी के हमले को रोका जाए, और कैसे खुद को मजबूत रखा जाए।

शुरुआत में, कायरा को बहुत मुश्किलें आईं। हर बार जब समीर उसे ट्रेनिंग के दौरान चुनौती देते, उसके पुराने डर सामने आ जाते। उसे उस घटना की यादें परेशान करतीं। पर समीर ने उसे बार-बार याद दिलाया कि वह उससे ज्यादा मजबूत है और उसे अपने भीतर की ताकत को पहचानना होगा। समीर के धैर्य और सपोर्ट से, कायरा धीरे-धीरे अपने डर को कम करने लगी।

समीर और कायरा की नजदीकी

समीर और कायरा के बीच सिर्फ कोच और छात्रा का संबंध नहीं रह गया था। धीरे-धीरे, कायरा ने महसूस किया कि समीर के साथ समय बिताते हुए उसे सुरक्षा और आत्मविश्वास का अनुभव हो रहा है। समीर न सिर्फ एक कोच थे, बल्कि वे कायरा के लिए एक दोस्त और मार्गदर्शक भी बन गए थे। समीर भी कायरा की दृढ़ इच्छाशक्ति और बदलाव की क्षमता से प्रभावित हुए बिना नहीं रह पाए। उनके बीच का यह गहरा संबंध दोस्ती से कुछ अधिक हो चला था।

समीर ने कई बार कोशिश की कि वह कायरा के लिए अपनी भावनाएं जाहिर करें, लेकिन वे जानते थे कि कायरा अभी एक नाजुक स्थिति में है। उन्हें उसके लिए सही समय का इंतजार करना था।

कायरा ने भी महसूस किया कि समीर के प्रति उसकी भावनाएं बदल रही हैं। लेकिन वह खुद को रोकती रही, क्योंकि वह नहीं चाहती थी कि उसके जीवन में कोई नया रिश्ता उसकी प्राथमिकता से ध्यान हटाए। उसकी सबसे बड़ी प्राथमिकता थी—खुद को मजबूत बनाना और अपने डर से पूरी तरह आज़ाद होना।

नारी शक्ति का जागरण:

एक दिन, कायरा का आत्मविश्वास अपने चरम पर था। वह अब उन दिनों की कायरा नहीं थी, जो हर किसी से डरती थी। समीर की ट्रेनिंग और उनकी बातें अब उसके खून में बस गई थीं। उसने ठान लिया था कि वह खुद के लिए और दूसरी लड़कियों के लिए एक उदाहरण बनेगी।

कायरा ने समीर से कहा, "तुम्हारे बिना मैं यह कभी नहीं कर पाती। तुमने मुझे सिखाया कि डर को भगाना कैसे है। अब मैं अपने लिए खड़ी हो सकती हूँ और दूसरों को भी सिखा सकती हूँ कि वे कैसे अपने डर को खत्म कर सकती हैं।"

समीर मुस्कुराते हुए बोले, "मैंने तुम्हें सिर्फ दिशा दी, कायरा। असली ताकत तुम्हारे भीतर थी।"

कायरा ने अपना एक सेल्फ डिफेंस क्लास शुरू किया, जहाँ वह लड़कियों और महिलाओं को आत्मरक्षा की ट्रेनिंग देती थी। वह अब एक प्रेरणा बन चुकी थी, खासकर उन महिलाओं के लिए जो किसी न किसी रूप में हिंसा का शिकार हुई थीं।

प्रेम का इज़हार:

एक दिन, जब समीर और कायरा एक ट्रेनिंग सेशन के बाद बैठकर बातें कर रहे थे, समीर ने अपनी भावनाओं को जाहिर करने का निर्णय लिया। उन्होंने कहा, "कायरा, मैं तुम्हारे संघर्ष, साहस, और बदलाव से बहुत प्रभावित हूँ। मैं हमेशा तुम्हारे साथ खड़ा रहूँगा, चाहे तुम मुझे अपने जीवन में दोस्त के रूप में चाहो या कुछ और।"

कायरा ने उसे देखा और उसके चेहरे पर एक मुस्कान खिल उठी। उसने कहा, "समीर, तुम मेरे जीवन में उस वक्त आए जब मुझे सबसे ज्यादा जरूरत थी। तुमने मुझे सिखाया कि मैं खुद के लिए लड़ सकती हूँ। और अब जब मैं मजबूत हूँ, मुझे लगता है कि मैं अपने दिल की बात सुन सकती हूँ। और मेरा दिल कहता है, मैं भी तुमसे प्यार करती हूँ।"

समीर ने कायरा का हाथ थाम लिया और दोनों ने साथ मिलकर एक नई शुरुआत का वादा किया—जहाँ उनका रिश्ता न सिर्फ प्यार, बल्कि एक दूसरे की इज्जत और समर्थन पर आधारित होगा।

कायरा और समीर की यह कहानी सिर्फ प्रेम की नहीं, बल्कि नारी शक्ति और आत्मरक्षा की महत्वपूर्णता की भी थी। दोनों ने मिलकर साबित किया कि सच्ची ताकत भीतर से आती है, और जब आत्मविश्वास होता है, तो हर डर को हराया जा सकता है।

50. Jeetal shah

Manav and Gungun, two distinct personalities residing in the same body, led a life that was a tapestry of concealed truths and fragmented memories. Manav, a diligent librarian by day, was the epitome of order and routine. His world was books and the quiet solace they provided. Gungun, on the other hand, emerged as the sun dipped below the horizon, a street artist whose vibrant murals breathed life into the sleepy town's walls.

Neither was aware of the other's existence, each believing they slept through the hours the other took over. This delicate balance persisted until one fateful evening when a peculiar book found its way into Manav's hands. It was a diary, the pages filled with tales of midnight escapades and colourful expressions of art, signed with a flourish - Gungun.

Intrigued and confused, Manav began to piece together the puzzle, staying awake through the night. As the clock struck twelve, he felt a familiar yet foreign surge of energy. The world around him shifted in hues and perspectives, and he found himself standing before a wall, paintbrush in hand, the name 'Gungun' echoing in his mind.

The story of Manav and Gungun is a journey of self-discovery, where the merging of day and night, order and chaos, leads to the realisation that they are but two sides of the same coin. Together, they learn to navigate the complexities of their shared existence, embracing the duality that makes them whole.

As they delved deeper into each other's lives, Manav and Gungun discovered that they had more in common than they initially thought. They both shared a love for art, though expressed in different forms. Manav found himself drawn to Gungun's colourful and bold street art, while Gungun admired Manav's meticulous attention to detail in his library work. Their collaboration on a mural brought them closer together, as they worked side by side, blending their unique styles into one cohesive piece. The town was abuzz with their creation, and people couldn't believe that the two artists were actually the same person. But as their bond grew stronger, so did the confusion within them. Manav struggled to maintain his routine and order while Gungun craved the freedom of expression and spontaneity. They were constantly at odds with each other, causing internal turmoil. It wasn't until they faced a crisis together that they truly understood the significance of their coexistence. A fire broke out in the library one night, and as Manav desperately tried to save the books, Gungun used his artistic skills to create a diversion and lead everyone to safety

51. Vivek Saswat

आगाज़

है धुआं सा कुछ यहां,
चिरागों को जलाते हैं,,
बदल दे कर लकीरों को,
कर खिलाफत जमाने से।

पकड़ ले बुलंदी की डोर हाथों में,
पंख कागजों की लगाके,,
नभ में खुद को उड़ाते हैं,
छा गया सहरसा अंधेरा है यहां।।

चल चिरागों को जलाते हैं,
बुझ गई है अब मशालें,,
रुकती सांसों से कुछ चिंगारी,
उधार लाते हैं,,
चल चिरागों को जलाते हैं।
चल चिरागों को जलाते हैं।।

विवेक शाश्वत...

52. Zainab Mustafa

LIFE IS A TRAIN NOT A STATION

15th of the 5th month in the year 2002, a train took off of its platform for its first ever journey.... Little did the captains knew, it was going to be one of the most exciting travels. It was an ordinary day, like the day before it and like the day that would come after. Not a drop different, the sun was rising as usual and the birds welcomed the daylight as usual; normal for all except the couple that welcomed their first born: a daughter. They held her as she started her journey wailing, terrified of all the destinations the train of her life would come across, eager to conquer each one of them, with the tiny breaths that the tiny soul took. As the day began, so did her life with a terrible sense of humor. It seemed like the train that had taken off just a few hours earlier, had already arrived to its first stop. The baby had Microphthalmia. I believe the weather got foggy after that, as none of the doctors could determine whether the girl would ever be able to see or not, living with the disability.

By nothing less than a miracle, the journey had resumed. The girl was now three years old and at the threshold of another stop in her trip. She had to start her education. Her parents were disheartened when specialists and consultants suggested the school for the blind. Ironically the same day, she started wearing thick glasses for her aid. After deeper consideration the parents gave her a chance at a regular school with children, who all in some way were not all like her, but all were trying to maintain their speed in crossing this platform. All their parents wanted them to live a regular life and yet still stand out in their individual journeys. Her parents and teachers held her hand at each of her wobbly steps, and even though she tripped sometimes, she found the right track eventually.

She dreamed of attending the same school as her sibling. And with that dream another stop had revealed itself in not a very good manner, her school had refused to let her continue with them in third grade. With their heads still high and full of optimism, the parents applied to her siblings' school even after receiving red flags for their decisions in relevance to her performance not being able to match her peers.

I guess it is true that the closing of a window, or a track, is the opening of a door or a new route because her dreams were now her reality as she entered a new place. Now she dreamed new dreams, with determination that one day, wIth enough efforts she will witness they come to life.

There is a theatrical beauty in train journeys. Sometimes when you look out of the windows you see clear hills and cheerful valleys; while sometimes you sit amicably still in the turbulence, watching storms raging outside. You have no choice but to accept the uncertainty, will the storm ever end? You never know but you can do nothing but hope.

I hope you understand I'm talking about life, specifically the life of our young dreamer. In a crowd, she always stood out because of her different eyes. Which meant dealing with questions and an unsurpassable urge of not being noticed. Her self-esteem crumbled at moments, but she held herself through the cracks. You see, You see, when a sword is broken and mended, it becomes stronger at the mended points. . She never let any of her weaknesses define her. Passing through storms do make you clean, and she did appear on the other side brighter and tougher with the ability to withstand the violence of storms.

When you look out of a window, you see your own reflection. At times it is blurry, but eventually you do see yourself, all of the grooves and crevices and curves and plains of your face. Exactly like that, one day

Our dreamer saw herself, in words and sentences, in prose and poetry. Where pain was beauty and ideas were freedom. She wanted to write stories of sceneries she had yet to see.

She did great things. Crossed stations that navigators had tagged impossible. Achieved everything doctors said she couldn't. Of course she would, there is a defiance in being a dreamer and she promised herself she would do greater.

As she traveled further, her journey took steeper turns. She decided at once she would memorize AL QURAN MAJEED. Immortalising her soul with the reverence of the holy text. It was an arduous journey in itself, but it was a journey to the stars. Every step was rougher than the last, but whenever she wavered the shine of the stars gave her strength to always move forward. To everyone's bewilderment, she completed her goal in one year. Now she dwelt among the stars that once gave her hope.

The girl completed college, consistently outperforming her peers and earning top honors. She overcame numerous obstacles and hardships but never gave up.

She is an authentic writer, and an author who has had her work published in books, magazines, and newspapers on a national and international scale.
Her goal is to earn a degree in English. She attended university, but there are still roadblocks in her path. Despite this, she is unstoppable in her pursuit of her goals. Would like a doctor with her name as pHD.

Destinations and stops along the way are fleeting. Despite her desire to continue basking in the glow of her success, she had decisions to make. She needed to go further, to establish a career. Unsurprisingly, it was difficult, few things in this life are not. Failure and rejection are unavoidable. The difference, however, is in the aftermath, in how determined you are to achieve your goals. Are we even mildly surprised that our dreamer has succeeded yet again despite criticism?
Changing paths is not a sign of weakness, but a sign of strength, that you trust yourself enough to go where your heart desires.
Even when the young girl's vision of dreams changed, her clarity of believing in them did not. I have said this before, life has a terrible sense of humour.

It's ironic that she couldn't physically see what was in front of her eyes without help, but in life she could see miles ahead; further than anyone her age could imagine. Life will continue to take her to too many stations, some of which she will want to live forever but knows she cannot. When everything around her is falling apart, the only thing holding her together is the hope that it will pass. It is often said that the only thing stronger than fear is hope. The only things that keep us going on this terrible lonely journey called life.

53. Janvi Pippal

DOLL

I lean against the wall, tears streaming down,
A fragile doll, lost in a world unbound.
I ask my life, "What's my fault?" it sneers,
"How much are you worth?" – a mocking spear.

In deep contemplation, I sit, like a glass doll ,
Questioning my own value, my heart downcast
A voice interrupts, shattering my thought,
"You sacrifice self-respect, moulding yourself like others want ."

A realization hit me hard, like morning's first light,
I've been a obedient doll ,dancing to others' wish.
Born to rule, but now I've lost my own voice,
A bruised doll, silenced by I noisy choice.

But now I rise, like a bud of flower
"No longer a doll, but a strong girl, I break through."
I shatter the mold, cast aside the pain,
Embracing self-worth, like a blooming flower's refrain.

My inner voice whispers, "Do you understand?"
I smile, with conviction, "I no longer anyone's doll"

54. सीमीं नईम सिद्दीक़ी

किसी के दिल में बसने का इरादा कर रहे हो तुम!
फंसाने और फंसने का इरादा कर रहे हो तुम।

चुनी है राह जो तुमने वहाँ आँसू ही आँसू हैं
कमाल ये है कि हँसने का इरादा कर रहे हो तुम।

अभी बेशक कली गुल हो लगेगी बाद में कांटा,
जिसे बाहों में कसने का इरादा कर रहे हो तुम।

निगल जाएगा वो तुमको समझ ये बाद आयेगा,
जिसे चाहत से डसने का इरादा कर रहे हो तुम।

ज़रा वक़्त और लेकर तुम उगो फूलों फलों, लेकिन!
मियां धरती में धंसने का इरादा कर रहे हो तुम।

खुशी तुमको नहीं भाती समझ हमको यही आता,
खुशी को ही तरसने का इरादा कर रहे हो तुम।

समेटों खुद में पहले तुम वो बदली बूंद का मौसम,
बिना मतलब बरसने का इरादा कर रहे हो तुम।

55. Radha Kumari

।। हम महिलाएं हैं ।।

हम महिलाएं हैं ,
और हम कभी कभी ये भूल जाते हैं कि हम पुरुष प्रधान समाज में रहते हैं,

हमारे लबों पे आने वाले मुस्कुराहट का,
और खुद को कभी सँवार लेने का,
सबका हिसाब देना होता है,

वरना समझा जाता है इसे जागीर अपने बाप की,
और करा दिया जाता है ये एहसास की रहना है स्त्री तुझे हमेशा सादा ही,
और तोड़ कर हमारे अरमानों को पटक दिया जाता है हमें धरा पर क्योंकि,

हम महिलाएं है,
और हम कभी कभी ये भूल जाते हैं कि हम पुरुष प्रधान समाज में रहते हैं।।

राधा कुमारी

56. Abismita Das

Unrecognised thoughts
— Abismita Das

Thoughts that Untie
those Knots of glimpses,
Trying to hold back something uncanny!
Into the backyard of Souvenir.
Tend to scream upon, just to say
Turn around love!
See, it's you. Seven years back
Whom you killed once & acted
As if she never existed for real

Soon after ,
Her heartbeat kept running. But
Those footsteps got stucked for a while
As if they want to stay and turn back!
Time passed, someone kept screaming
From the behind,
She stayed but not moved
Slowly slowly, screams felt like honey
The dark room, whispered
She might turn a bit, now!

Who knows what's her next move?
She smiled & said,
Who knows, it's the honey or the honeybee
That may live a sting again
This time, may be
Deeper than the old one
That killed the 'old her' seven years ago!

All night,in the dark room
She stayed, she smiled, she talked
but she never turned behind again!

57. Runa

Loving him is like holding onto a secret that only I know.
There are when I find myself smiling
just because I thought of him.
I've spent countless nights replaying memories
the way his voice sounds,
the way his eyes light up

It's hard, sometimes, loving him like this
from a distance, in silence.
I see him go about his day, talk to others,
and I wonder if he's ever thought of me the same way.
But then I remind myself that it doesn't matter.
Loving him has become a part of who I am.

I don't need him to know.
I don't need him to say anything back.
Just knowing he's there, living his life,
is enough to make me happy.
I write poems about him
the way he makes me feel,
the way his presence alone
brings a sense of calm I can't explain.

Maybe one day I'll be able to tell him,
but for now, I'm okay with loving him quietly.
I'm okay with keeping this feeling to myself,
because loving him, even in silence,
feels better than not loving him at all.
—@talesbyruna

58. Kiran Rathod

THE HOLLOW LEFT

One day, if I ever start bleeding, go away.
Finding the faults in me will pave the way.
I would never want to hurt a heart like you,
So don't worry, I won't make you stay.

Never did I thought it would come to THIS.
All the joys wil be amiss
But something broke in me recently
Now I just wait for the dooms bliss

My lungs are filled with void, warm and hollow,
The burning in me is to keep me alive, so I just swallow
Maybe as you said I should have changed
But biting the bullet Is something I don't follow

Life goes with anything but flow
Why doesn't it let me grow
At peace where warmth is everywhere
To breath easily without a care.

things I did was indeed for me
Of course the result was not all glee
But I do wanted this somewhere
I really wanted to see me

But again it's not your fault
It has always been me
All the solutions in the world
But they are blaming all me.

59. Rudra

Whispers Of Horizon

Stumbled upon a lighthouse
With many questions that arose,
Searching for answers,
Beyond the horizon of the sea,
Taking only a breath to sigh...

Leftover feelings are fleeting,
Moments of joy are expunging,
Time passes like the wind,
Lonely feet entangled and bind.

Houses of sand break with each wave,
A child's dream, it shatters,
Water kisses the feet of stone,
A beautiful scenery nature has claimed as its own.

May this disturbed soul find peace,
While taking everything at risk,
Awareness, a fool, gone for a while,
Take this chance to enjoy in time.

60. Sangeeta Jolly

Festival Fusion of India.

India, a land of vibrant cultures and rich traditions, is renowned for its myriad festivals celebrated throughout the world. These festivals, each unique in its significance and customs, collectively reflect the country's profound cultural heritage. As diverse as they are, they also represent a beautiful fusion of tradition and modernity, creating tepestry of celebration that transcends regional and cultural boundaries.

Culturall Melting Pot

India's festivals are a testament to its diversity from the grand festival of Diwali, Holi and Eid to the regional celebration like Pongal, Baisakhi, and Onam, each festival carries its own story rituals and significance. However what stands out is how these festivals, while rooted in distinct traditions, often overlap and influence one another. For instance Diwali and Eid though representing different religions backgrounds both feature grand feasts and community gatherings that foster a spirit of unity and celebration.

Modern Twists on Traditions

In Contemporary India, traditional festivals are increasingly being celebrated with modern twist. For instance, vibrant street parties during Holi have evolved to include eco- friendly colours and themes of sustainability,, Similarly, Diwali celebrations non often incorporate themes of digital connectivity and social media, with online greetings and virtual celebrations becoming common place.

Unity in Diversity

The concept of unity in diversity is vividly illustrated during festivals when people from different backgrounds come together. During major festivals like Ganesh Chaturthi in Mumbai or Durga Puja in Kolkata, the entire city often participates, regardless of their individual religious or cultural affiliations. This collective celebration highlights a shared identity and common joy that transcends individual differences.

61. Ankit Kumar Singh

Bhagwatgita or Bhagwat + Gita means " A song of God" . This song was sung 5000 years ago by the Godhead of supreme personality lord Shri Krishna in a capacity of teacher, friend and cousin to Student Arjuna(one of the five Pandavas) . Bhagwatgita is a manual of Life. For example - If we purchase any product then we also receive its manual. Manual is just set of guidelines to be followed for smooth functioning of a product and therefore we could enjoy the results of product in best possible way. In same way bhagwatgita is a manual of Life or say oxygen of life. This nectar has to be taken earliest so that all students irrespective of their academic status, job status, salary status and life status could be happy and sound.

Think , what will happen, if the warranty of the purchased product expires and then you read its manual? Similarly, Bhagwatgita is not a subject to be taken at old age. It will be of no use. Another example - Suppose a " APP DEVELOPER" develops "XYZ" app. Now again think, Who will be the best suitable person to give guidelines to users for proper use , maintenance, do's and don'ts, etc related to app? Your answer will be " APP DEVELOPER" . Similarly Supreme creator of this entire creation has bestowed upon the purpose of his creation, proper use , maintenance, do's and don'ts, etc in a manual called Bhagwatgita.

PRESENT DROWNING SITUATION FOR THE STUDENTS -

1. In this fast running volatile material world, after birth , all of us face our true identity crisis
that is who we are , why we are here, purpose of our arrival on this globe , etc . Maximum
Knowledge that we receive is only limited around material gain that is how to come only first
in class , how to get selected for best packages, best possible way for material accumulation.
There is no class , school for mental happiness, eternal happiness, satisfaction and peace.

2. Since we are conditioning our future only for material accumulation, competitiveness, higher
social and family status, therefore the result is anxiety, stress, depression, sexual violence
(acid attacks) old age home culture, hate crimes, creating set of human robots having huge
deficit in personality development, humanity and merits.

3. 50-100 years back from now, there was no concept of SUICIDE in Indian context. But now suicide has become fashion and heroic practice. Academic failure (Even in school), failure in competitive exams, jobs failure, married life failure, family life failure or any reason takes oneself towards suicidal rope instantly.

4. Unsolved National issues- Corruption, terrorism, poverty , law and order issues, Climate Change, Economic crisis, National physical and mental health issues, population explosion, Pollution, cybersecurity, natural and human made disasters,etc . All these outstanding issues originated when we lost our original identity, purpose of this alloted human body and somehow sever deficit in personality development supportive to National growth.

5 . Collective reason of all problems are deficit in true knowledge and everything around is functioning on " HOW " or say just rituals and process are followed. No efforts to convert HOW into "WHY" or say purpose behind.

BHAGWATGITA AS MASTERSTROKE TO ALL THE PROBLEMS -

1. It solves our identity crisis issues that we all are Souls and not body. For sometime and for some specific purpose we are alloted this auspicious human body. We have to attain material knowledge for material accumulation but keep SPIRITUAL KNOWLEDGE as its base.

2. When we read , understand and implement bhagwatgita in our day to day life situations, we get potential to deal all Worldly issues. We are free from anxiety, depression, sexual violence, Old age home culture, hate crimes and humanity is restored as our outlook is changed now. We will see everyone around as soul that is energy of God interacting us and not body. Therefore we will develop natural respect, compassion, love and peace for everyone.

3. All the Western educational institutions such as universities and schools are adding Bhagwatgita in their management, classes from top to bottom to counter all the outstanding issues specifically centred to stress, anxiety, depression and suicide. And also to change outlook from GREAT ECONOMIC DEVELOPMENT TO GREAT HUMANITY LED PERSONALITY DEVELOPMENT. Every institute should have this department for spiritual development an eliminate KOTA SUICIDAL HOTSPOTS in our country.

4. When someone is in true knowledge of bhagwatgita, he/ she realises that Supreme Lord Krishna resides in everyone's heart and noting our karmic accounts. Therefore, there will be natural resistance for practicing corruption, increase in physical and mental well-being, decline in law and order issues, women issues. Bhagwatgita can also solve issues related to Climate Change, population explosion and pollution.

5. Bhagwatgita changes our outlook from HOW to WHY., PROCESS TO PURPOSE. This will give Paradigm shift in our life , inculcating rational thinking and scientific temperament.

GREAT PERSONALITIES FOLLOWED/ FOLLOWING BHAGWATGITA -

1. DR. A.P. J. Abdul Kalam (Bhagwatgita - inspiration for Agni 5 series missiles)
2. Dr. Homi jhangir bhabha (Bhagwatgita - source for Indian nuclear research program)
3. Dr. Vikram sarabhai (Bhagwatgita - source for Indian space research program)
4. Issac Newton (Bhagwatgita - source of gravitational theory)
5. Albert Einstein (Bhagwatgita - source of time relativity theory)
6. Mahatma Gandhi ji (Independence movement strategy source - bhagwatgita)
7. NASA 's source for space lead - bhagwatgita
8. Honourable prime minister Shri Narendra Modi ji (inspiration - bhagwatgita)
9. J.Robert Oppenheimer (nuclear bomb- idea, inspiration source - bhagwatgita)
10. Mark Zuckerberg (success source - bhagwatgita)
11. Ford car company (head success bhagwatgita)
12. Steve jobs (founder apple inspiration - bhagwatgita)
13. E Shreedharan (Metro man of India, source - bhagwatgita)

MANY MORE..... LIST IS INFINITE

62. Sakshi Singh

Vo ek din jab muche dhunta aayega
Me agar na mili, to kithar jayega

Shayad vo sitaron se mera rasta poochega,
Ya chandni raaton mein bhatakta phirega.

Vo hawao se meri khushboo talashega,
Ya baarish ki boondon mein mujhe dhondega.

Shayad yaadon ke jungle mein bhatakta phirega,
Yaa khwabon mein aakar mujhe pukarega,

Agar phir bhi mujhko woh paa na sakaa,
To shayad meri tasveer se baatein karega.

Bato hi baato me halat jo mere puchega,
Me agar tanha kahu to phir kya karega??

Vo ek din jab muche dhunta aayega
Me agar na mili, to kithar jayega ?

63. Dinesh Poswal

"गुर्जर आरक्षण "

आरक्षण के खातिर
लड़ी लड़ाई सरकार
को यह बात
रास न आई ।।1।।

पटरी व सड़कों
पर जाम लगाया
आरक्षण के खातिर
लहू बहाया और
गुर्जर जाति का
इतिहास बनाया ।।2।।

जब कर्नल बाबा
का साथ पाया,
मलाणा डुंगर पर
जाम लगाया और
आंदोलन को सफल बनाया ।।3।।

64. Aadithyaa

Poem Title - Bleeding Love

Sucked the soul of the pretty Dried them to the flesh Licked her sorrow like a wound And sealed it with a kiss Let her believe in love While I justify my lust She's not gonna leave Because I burdened her with trust Her body waited for my touch And I felt it when I was home And used her for the features While I slutted like a whore Now, she came with a warning Love me to death or kill me with the knife I took the knife away and apologized And just hugged her with a smile Then, slowly felt her face And closed those perfect eyes So she couldn't see the face of love Which felt her oozing blood tonight

65. Surender Singh Rathore

RAO SIHAJI'S UNTOLD STORY As the Sun was shining PROUDLY in the sky that day, casting a warm, amber glow across the golden sands of Rajasthan, the Mehrangarh Fort in Jodhpur stood proudly against the golden light. Its towering walls, a formidable blend of red sandstone and intricate carving, loomed like ancient guardians of a bygone era. Why did I say that the sun shone PROUDLY? Well, that's because it was built by the Rathores of Mandore, who are descendants of Sun (Suryavanshi Clan). Mehrangarh's literal meaning is 'The land of descendants of the Sun'. In the heart of the Thar Desert, the Mehrangarh fort is not just a historical monument or a tourist place; it is a testament to the indomitable spirit of the Rajput kings who ruled these lands for centuries. The fort seems to carry thousands of untold stories; some are known to mankind, but most of them are long forgotten or never mentioned. We'll talk about one such story here today; it might fascinate you guys a lot, or maybe you won't even believe it. The story is of the founding member of Rathores in Rajasthan (the first one). This clan moved to Rajasthan in the 12th century, and before that, they were ruling in Kannauj (Uttar Pradesh) and even in the South too, with a different name (Rashtrakut) and at a different time. The story is of Rao Sihaji, son of Rao Setrav ji (King of Kannauj). The folklore tells us that Rao Setrav ji had a child after a very long time, so he told the midwife to mark a line on the ground where the shadow of the sun falls at that time to mark the time of birth of the child and prepare his kundli (for astrology purposes), but she forgot to do so because she went on to tell everyone about the celebrations and distribute sweets to everyone in the palace, etc. When she got reminded of it, a lot of time had already elapsed, but just so the king wouldn't get angry with her, she carved a line at that time where the shadow of the sun fell (which was actually wrong), but she did it anyway just to keep herself safe and sound. The next day, the best pandits, brahmins, and jyotish (astrologers) were called from all over the state, doing their calculations to prepare the kundli, but even after a very long time, none of them prepared one as they were all looking pale, shocked, and confused altogether. Upon being questioned by the king again and again, one of them told the king that his son's nakshatra (kundli) is in such a way that if the king sees his son's face, the king won't be alive for long. The king was shocked to know this, and with a heavy heart, he ordered his butchers to kill the child. The group of butchers came, but they felt sympathy toward the child. Sympathy, you ask? because the butchers are supposed to kill in cold blood, right? Well, fate and destiny were playing their roles at that time. So the butchers decided not to kill the child themselves but instead to leave the child in the forest so some animal would eat it and the blood of an infant wouldn't be on their hands (I don't know how the latter was justifiable to their conscience if not the former). So they went to the jungle and found a lion's den. They placed the child at the entrance, and it rolled inside the den because of the steepness at the entrance. Well, the den was of a lioness (instead of a lion, because that's what we assumed earlier), and she just gave birth to a cub (some of you might know that lioness, after giving birth, faints for several hours due to pain during labor, and that's what had happened at that time). She fainted, and the child got mixed up with the cub. When the lioness woke up, she saw two kids—one cub and one human child—but assumed that they were both hers and started feeding them her milk. Over the years, the child grew and was walking and running just like other lions on all four limbs, with nails and hair overgrown. He was also playing and hunting with other lions (just like lions usually do). And here in Rajasthan's Pali district, the Paliwals (a tribe of rich locals) were constantly being targeted, looted, and harassed by local thieves, dacaits, and were literally being terrorized by them. They asked for help from a Bhati from the nearby state of Jaisalmer. The Bhati suggested that they go to Kannauj to find the solution to their problem (the Bhati was a spiritual man who had a divine thought about this). So accordingly, following his guidance, the Paliwals went to Kannauj to meet the king there and ask for his help. On the way to the palace of Kannauj, they encountered something very unusual. While going through the forest path, they saw a human roaming with lions as a part of their pack. The human was playing, running, and hunting with lions, and yet none of them attacked that human. The paliwals were shocked to see this, and when they reached the palace, they narrated the whole incident to the king about the jungle and their problem as well. Now one of the very same butchers who kept the child at the entrance of the cave a few years ago was passing nearby and heard the whole story as it was being described by paliwals to the king. Now the butcher thought that their secret would be out (that they didn't do what the king ordered them to do in the first place and instead left the kid inside the cave). And he knew in his heart that this human with lions is the very same child whom they left in the cave all those years ago. So in order to keep himself alive, he asked for forgiveness from the king and told him the whole truth behind the story. The king forgave him for knowing the whole story. Upon hearing it completely, the king immediately ordered some of his best troops, especially archers, to go on a hunt to 'hunt down' his kid, his successor, and bring him back to the palace where he belonged. Then the hunt began, and they found the 'lion pack', and one of the archers shot an arrow laced with sedatives, and it hit the target—the kid. He fell down immediately (just injured and unconscious, not killed). The rest of the lions ran away, leaving behind the 'human lion'. They picked his body up, stowed it on the back of a horse, and rode back to the palace, where they gave the boy a makeover. They cut his overgrown hair and nails, etc., and taught him how to walk, talk, and behave like a human. He was taught the way of fighting too. The training went on for quite some time. After all those years, the kid became an adult with a strong physique and huge muscles (as he drank the milk of a lioness for most of his childhood years, and maybe the Hindi idiom 'sherni ka doodh piya hai' originated from here). The paliwals requested the king send that very boy, Rao Sihaji—Siha means the one who drank the milk of a sinhni (lioness). To send aid to the Paliwals, the king agreed and sent Sihaji to Pali, Rajasthan. In return, the paliwals promised that Sihaji would be recognized as their king there and that he would be paid taxes in order to provide them security. Upon reaching Pali, Sihaji fought against those local dacaits, killed them all, and freed the Paliwals from their agony. But the paliwals got greedy, as they thought that now that no more dacaits are alive to harass them, why to recognize Sihaji as their Rao (king)? By doing so, they could save a lot of money from being paid as taxes too. So they went against their word and refused him the throne. In return, Rao Sihaji warned them that if they didn't honor their word, he would have to fight against them to claim what is rightfully his (otherwise, if he hadn't come here to provide aid to paliwals, he would have been the next king of Kannauj, and he gave up his title there to help them). The Paliwals didn't agree, and thus began the war. Sihaji went on a war against them and claimed his right to the 'newly built throne'. Now, to tell you about the magnitude of the people killed in that war, we will try a different approach. Paliwals used to wear janeyu, a sacred thread worn around the shoulder of a person, usually by brahmins. Now the janeyu from the dead bodies of paliwals was removed, and that weighed 2.5 quintals, i.e., 250 kilograms. I'm just wondering how many Paliwals would have been killed so their janeyu could weigh that much. It's unbelievable! It was complete bloodshed—an annihilation. After the carnage, he established his rule over there and continued to expand his territories. After a few generations, the Mandore fort was gifted to his family in the form of dowry by the

Pratihar Clan for matrimonial relations with Rao Chunda (king of that time) of the Rathore clan, and they shifted their capital to Mandore. Later, the capital was again shifted to present-day Jodhpur to strategically enhance their defense. The state of Marwar kept on growing to such an extent that it became the most powerful state of Rajputana in its prime, especially under the rule of Rao Jodha and Rao Maldeo. Now you must be thinking that this is just the plain history of a clan; what's so mind-boggling about this? Well, let me tell you some interesting parts. Most of you might have heard about Rudyard Kipling. No? Well, he's the writer of 'The Jungle Book. In this book, there's a character named Mowgli; yes, most of us know about this character. Now you might have noticed some similarities between the childhood stories of Mowgli and Rao Sihaji (they both spent some years in the jungle while growing up). Now comes the twist: Rudyard Kipling visited the Mehrangarh fort in 1890 and saw a painting of a human playing with lions while being in their pack. So he asked a local about it, and the local, who was of the same Rathore family, told Rudyard Kipling the whole story of Rao Sihaji (the founder of the Rathore clan in Rajasthan) and his childhood and how this painting depicts his childhood. Rudyard Kipling was amazed to know this, and after some time he returned to London, and in 1892 came the first draft of the story, which later got published worldwide in 1894. Rudyard Kipling and Disney printed books and made movies on the story; they both became worldwide hits and earned millions and millions from it, but no one ever mentioned from where the story originated, thus no recognition. Now you must be thinking, How do I know all this? Well, I belong to the very same family of Rathores, whose ancestry tree goes all the way back to Rao Sihaji, Shri Ram (Lord Rama), the Ikshvaku clan, and Suryadev himself (the Sun). - Surender Singh Rathore.

66. Abhishek Yadav

THE MAN Man, the soldier in the storm, Stands weary, though his heart stays warm, He faces battles out of sight, Endures alone, no end in sight. From boyhood taught to be the rock, To never tremble, never knock, On doors that promise comfort's touch, For men are told they need not much. But deep within, the rivers swell, With unshed tears, the stories tell, Of dreams abandoned, hopes long lost, Behind his strength, a heavy cost. He walks a path that's seldom clear, Shoulders the burdens year by year, For every triumph bears its toll, Each silent cry chips at his soul. Yet who will notice, who will care? For men are meant to simply bear, The weight of worlds upon their back, To fill the void, to bridge the lack. And when they falter, when they fall, They're asked to rise, stand straight, stand tall, To brush aside the creeping fears, And carry on, despite the tears. But what if man could show his pain, Let fall the mask that's worn in vain? To be embraced, not just for might, But for his courage in the night. For strength is not in stoic stance, But in the power to advance, To speak the words, to break the chain, And free himself from silent strain. Imagine if the world could see, The soldier's vulnerability, And offer not just praise for fight, But comfort in his darkest night. To tell the man it's safe to rest, That human hearts, though tough, are blessed With grace to feel, with space to cry, To ask for help, and question why. For men, too, seek a hand to hold, A heart to hear the truths untold, A space to break, to breathe, to mend, To know they need not just defend. So let the walls of silence break, For every man, for every ache, Deserves a voice, a hand, a friend, A chance to heal, a path to bend. Man, the soldier of this life, Is more than just the sum of strife. He's heart, he's soul, he's flesh and bone, And he should never walk alone. So may we offer peace and care, To every man who's fought despair, And let them know they're not alone, In this long fight, this life they've known. For every wound, both seen and not, Each unspoken battle fought, Let's stand beside the men we love, And lift them high, not just above.

67. Gulam subhani

Rose petals scatter like blessings on the wind, Aromaticizing the air with it's scent throughout the surrounding. One sudden blow freed the rose petals apart, And carried them to the serenity of that beautiful girl's heart. She picked those petals & carried them along; Cause she was collecting them for the marriage ceremony to come. While she was stepping along the garden she came across a men, She stumbled upon him & all the petals flied in the air; Before she might fall the ma hold her in his arms, And the falling petals made the scene for a beautiful romance. ~Gulam Subhani

68. Aaradhana Aiyyar

Adolescence - By Aaradhana Aiyyar A time to grow physically, mentally and socially, And to dress, speak or behave boastfully. Dread the time or take solace of your teenage Your change from kid to adult passes through this stage. O pen up about yourself or be reserved, Choice is yours that is you deserve L earn from the mistakes you make It is the risk you have to take. E everything might be wrong or be right But at the end of the tunnel will always be a light. S colding from our parents is a daily routine, But it is to bring us to discipline. C arrears to decide, exams to take, That keep us fully awake. E veryone does not turn into a friend Many will turn into someone you will resent. N ot a single party to miss, not a day without social media, But isn't that our euphoria? C ome on! Enjoy your time while you can, Cause after becoming an adult you'll be cooking food in a pan. E Nd your adolescence with no regrets and set records hard to break, So even your adolescence misses you and wants to have a double take. First find a likely place, A place to haunt Where every adolescent will be undaunt.

69. Aditi Bodhankar

Title: Not My Mother

In another world, my mother is free, Not bound by the life that was chosen for me. She follows her dreams, her heart's silent call, In a place where she rises, she doesn't just fall. She steps into college, her future in sight, A bright, shining path filled with hope and light. She travels to places she's longed to explore, In markets of spices and on foreign shores. In France, she captures the beauty around, With laughter and joy, in moments profound. She tastes every dish, finds warmth in the new, In this world, she blossoms, her spirit breaks through. Maybe in Japan, beneath cherry trees, She dances in spring with the soft, gentle breeze. She meets someone special, a partner in dreams, Together they wander, unraveling seams. In another world, she breathes life so deep, With no regrets to haunt her, no promises to keep. She lives in the now, her heart wide and true, In this life unchosen, she finds something new.

Yet here I am, in a world filled with pain, Wondering what could have been, wishing in vain. For in her freedom, I see what I miss, A mother who lived, not just existed in bliss. In her eyes, I see stories of courage and grace, A glimpse of her laughter, the light on her face. Though I am her daughter, in dreams we may part, Her journey inspires the strength in my heart. In another life, she dances with stars, But here, I hold her, no matter the scars. Her spirit, my guide, through shadows and light, In every step forward, she shines ever bright.

70. Drishti Engineer

The Power of Big Data Big data is a widely used and powerful technology. Now the next set of questions you'll be having are: What is Big Data? Is it useful to learn this technology? Why is everyone talking about it? Well big data is a phrase that depicts the large volume of data – both structured and unstructured. That engulfs businesses on a day-to-day basis. The amount of data isn't important. Important is what organizations decide to do with the data. Big data can be studied for insights that give rise to better decisions and strategic business moves. History of big data: The phrase Big data indicates to data that is huge, fast or complex. So much that it's difficult or impossible to process using traditional methods. The act of retrieving and storing huge amounts of information for analytics has been around for a long time. Although, the concept of big data gained momentum in the early 2000s Need of big data The importance as well as need of big data doesn't revolve around the amount of data you have, but what you do with it. Data can be taken from any source and be analyzed. To find answers that allow: 1) cost reductions 2) time reductions 3) new product development and optimized offerings 4) smart decision making. Applications of big data: Big data is being used in various fields to get some insight. Fields like banking, agriculture, chemistry, data mining, cloud computing, finance, marketing, stocks, healthcare, etc. The healthcare sector has lagged behind other sectors in the usage of big data, part of the problem arises from resistance to change providers are accustomed to making treatment decisions independently. Using their own clinical judgment, rather than relying on rules based on big data. Technologies you need to know to make a future in the field of big data: NoSQL is crucial part of big data and databases that support NoSQL thus become important as well. Cassandra and MongoDB are the two most commonly used NoSQL databases. Hadoop, Hive and Apache Spark are the prominent tools used to analyze data. There are other tools available as well like Rapid Miner, Apache Storm and so on. Programming languages like R are also common. Big data challenges faced today: With the ever-increasing number of IOT devices and the gigabytes and petabytes of data they generate it's hard to manage, store and analyze this data. Thus, making it one of the most common challenge faced by Big data. Dealing with huge amounts of data is one but migrating these existing data workloads to a platform where analysis can be performed on it is also considered as a challenge. As you don't want to avoid errors and loss of data and dealing with huge amounts of it we always run a risk of losing some of it.

We also need powerful streaming data pipelines. Pipelines that are elastic enough to take the data and load it properly. These datasets are large and scaling it can be a challenge. In order to analyze this data, we need to deploy some sort of machine learning algorithm. The job has to be done properly if some data is dropped it can influence the results.

Roles that must be included to make a big data organization successful: Good Data engineers are required to build pipelines that fetch clean data. A Decision maker who decides how far you want to go with your data driven application. An analyst to explore the data and get insights and potential relations which can be useful in ML model. Applied Machine learning Engineers who have real world experience building production ML models from latest and best information by the researchers. Data scientists who have mastery over statistics and ML. Analytics manager who can lead the team. Social scientists and ethicists who ensure that quantitative impact is there for the project you're working on and is the right thing to do. All there play an important role in making a big data organization successful. Thus, they need to work together in harmony. All of these people are not actually required to make a big data organization successful. One person can take up two to three roles at once. Conclusion: Big Data is a powerful tool that makes things ease in various fields as said above. Big data applications are applied in various fields like banking, agriculture, chemistry, data mining, cloud computing, finance, marketing, stocks, healthcare, etc. - Drishti Engineer Reference: https://www.sas.com/en_us/insights/big-data/what-is-big-data.html

71. Anmol Agarwal
The Forgotten Melody

In a small, sleepy town nestled between rolling hills, there was a house that had stood untouched for decades. It wasn't particularly grand or imposing, but it carried with it an aura of mystery, for no one had set foot inside since the last resident, a reclusive musician named Elara, disappeared without a trace. Some said she left to find inspiration for her unfinished symphony, while others whispered of darker, inexplicable things. The town's children were warned not to venture near the house, but like all forbidden things, it held an irresistible allure. One summer afternoon, Maya, a curious and adventurous girl with a love for old stories, found herself standing before the house. The once vibrant blue shutters had faded to a dull grey, and vines twisted around the stone walls like nature's attempt to reclaim what had been abandoned. Her heart pounded as she pushed open the gate, its creak slicing through the thick silence. Stepping onto the porch, Maya hesitated before pressing her hand against the weathered wooden door. To her surprise, it swung open effortlessly, revealing a world frozen in time. Dust hung in the air like fine mist, and the faint scent of parchment and wood filled her nose.

The room was small, cluttered with papers and scattered sheets of music. A grand piano stood in the center, its keys yellowed with age. Drawn to it, Maya walked over, her fingers brushing the cool ivory. She had heard stories of Elara's music, how it could make people feel things they didn't even know they were capable of feeling. But no one had ever heard the final piece she had been working on. As Maya sat down at the piano, she noticed a single sheet of music lying on the stand. The notes were strange, unfamiliar, but something about them called to her. She placed her fingers on the keys and began to play. The melody that flowed from the piano was hauntingly beautiful, a combination of sorrow and hope intertwined in every note. It was as if the music held memories, stories untold, and emotions long forgotten. The room seemed to come alive with the sound, the air vibrating with an energy that made the hair on the back of her neck stand up. Suddenly, the temperature dropped.

The light streaming through the window dimmed, and a soft voice whispered in the air, "You found it." Maya stopped playing, her heart racing. She looked around the room, but no one was there. The voice was soft, almost like a breath, yet it felt familiar. She placed her hands back on the keys, and as she resumed the melody, the figure of a woman slowly appeared beside her—ethereal, translucent, yet undeniably real. It was Elara. Her face was serene, but her eyes were filled with a longing that Maya couldn't quite understand. The ghostly figure moved toward the piano, her fingers hovering just above Maya's hands as if guiding her. Together, they played the melody, and the house, long forgotten by the world, seemed to pulse with life once more. When the final note echoed into silence, Elara smiled. "Thank you," she whispered, her form beginning to fade. "Wait!" Maya called out. "What happened to you?" Elara's smile lingered as she dissolved into the air, leaving behind only the soft, lingering sound of the forgotten melody. Maya sat in silence for a long time, the weight of the moment pressing against her chest. She didn't know what had just happened, but she knew one thing for certain: Elara's music, her final creation, had found its way into the world at last. And in that moment, Maya realized that some stories, some melodies, were never truly forgotten—they were simply waiting for the right person to hear them.

72. Kirti Gupta

How 'Stay Interviews' are the New Exit Interviews In the current era of advanced corporate concerns, organizations have come to the understanding that the primary objective of understanding people does not lie in how to address their exit but rather finding out why one does not strategize on leaving the organization. This has informed the young age rise in the concept of proactive interviews as this one allows guesses on "stay interviews" asking workers their thoughts, getting their views in a more constructive and psychological way than more conventional exit interviews which only deal with the aftermath. It is no secret that exit interviews have been utilized to evaluate the causes of employee turnover, but such interventions are not practical since they are institutive after the fact. Conversely, stay interviews occur when the employee is still in good standing with the organization, giving managers the opportunity to reveal possible dissatisfaction before it gets worse. This encourages a much more productive feedback cycle which allows for the change of policies that would otherwise lead to high employee attrition and enhance the satisfaction of the remaining staff. It is no secret that exit interviews have been utilized to evaluate the causes of employee turnover, but such interventions are not practical since they are institutive after the fact. Conversely, stay interviews occur when the employee is still in good standing with the organization, giving managers the opportunity to reveal possible dissatisfaction before it gets worse. This encourages a much more productive feedback cycle which allows for the change of policies that would otherwise lead to high employee attrition and enhance the satisfaction of the remaining staff. It is no secret that exit interviews have been utilized to evaluate the causes of employee turnover, but such interventions are not practical since they are institutive after the fact. Conversely, stay interviews occur when the employee is still in good standing with the organization, giving managers the opportunity to reveal possible dissatisfaction before it gets worse. This encourages a much more productive feedback cycle which allows for the change of policies that would otherwise lead to high employee attrition and enhance the satisfaction of the remaining staff. Stay interviews are advantageous for the management as they enhance the development of leadership skills. They enhance relationships with the team, help appreciate the underlying reasons for each member's pursuit of specific goals and promote a more humane stance towards management. In the end, this nurtures a more team-oriented environment at the workplace. Stay interviews are advantageous for the management as they enhance the development of leadership skills. They enhance relationships with the team, help appreciate the underlying reasons for each member's pursuit of specific goals and promote a more humane stance towards management. In the end, this nurtures a more team-oriented environment at the workplace.

73. Shubham Singhal

In a bustling, modern city where high-rises gleamed and technology intertwined with daily life, the Kapoor family was nestled in a comfortable apartment. They lived in an upscale neighborhood, and to the outside world, they appeared to be thriving—a loving couple, successful careers, and now, a newborn. But within the walls of that sleek home, the atmosphere was suffocating. The day Riya was born, the mood in the family soured. Her father, Raj Kapoor, had yearned for a son, a successor to carry on the family name, someone to share in his achievements. Her mother, Meera, though more compassionate, feared the societal stigma attached to raising a daughter in a family that so openly preferred a boy. Riya was swaddled in blankets of disdain, and instead of being welcomed into a world of love, she was met with cold, indifferent glares. As Riya grew, the rejection became her constant companion. Her older brother, Arjun, was showered with affection, pride, and attention. Every time he scored a goal in football or brought home a perfect report card, the house buzzed with celebrations. In contrast, Riya's achievements were met with silence or quick dismissals. When she won a poetry competition at school, her father didn't even look up from his newspaper, and her mother only offered a strained smile. At school, things were no better. Word of her family's disregard for her had spread. Children are often cruel in their ignorance, and Riya became the target of their taunts. "Daddy's disappointment," they would sneer, laughing as they pulled at her hair or pushed her books out of her hands. Even the teachers seemed to overlook her, more interested in the popular, affluent kids who didn't carry the invisible weight of familial rejection. For years, Riya's life followed this oppressive rhythm. She spent most of her time alone, immersing herself in books, her only escape. The words she read filled her with a sense of longing for a world where she could be loved and appreciated. She developed a passion for writing, pouring her feelings into poetry and short stories, but she never dared share them with her family. By the time she reached her teenage years, Riya's home life had worsened. Her father, disappointed that she wasn't excelling in the ways he expected, began to verbally berate her. He would remind her, in no uncertain terms, that she was a burden, an unwanted responsibility. "If only you had been a boy," he would mutter, loud enough for her to hear. Her mother, while slightly more protective, did little to intervene, trapped in the fear of defying her husband. Despite the rejection, Riya carried a quiet strength within her. She focused on her studies and excelled academically, determined to find a way out of the suffocating life she was living. She had dreams of leaving the city, going to university, and starting a life where she could be free of the toxic expectations that shackled her. When she was 18, Riya received a scholarship to attend a prestigious university in another city. It was her chance at freedom, but the moment was bittersweet. When she announced the news at home, her father scoffed. "You think you're going to make something of yourself out there? Don't waste your time. You'll never be as successful as your brother." Her mother offered a weak, "That's good, Riya," but it was clear no one believed in her potential. Undeterred, Riya left for university with nothing but her suitcase, her savings, and the fire of determination burning in her heart. For the first time in her life, she was free. At university, she found solace in like-minded individuals, especially in her writing courses. She blossomed, her professors recognizing her talent and encouraging her to publish her work. But the scars of her childhood lingered. Riya found it difficult to trust people, always fearing rejection. She avoided relationships, both romantic and platonic, too afraid to let anyone too close. That changed in her final year of university when she met Arjun—strangely, the same name as her brother, though this Arjun was nothing like him. Arjun was in her creative writing class, a quiet, thoughtful man with an easy smile. He admired Riya's work, often staying behind after class to discuss her poetry with her. At first, Riya kept him at arm's length, convinced that someone like him couldn't truly be interested in her, but over time, his genuine kindness broke through her defenses. One evening, as they sat together in the campus coffee shop, Arjun asked her about her family. Riya hesitated. She had never told anyone the full story of her upbringing, but with Arjun, she felt safe. So, she opened up, sharing the years of neglect, the bullying, and the sense of being unwanted. Tears stung her eyes as she spoke, but she didn't hold back. When she finished, Arjun didn't offer empty platitudes or tell her that things would have been different if he had been there. He simply took her hand and said, "You deserved better. And none of it was your fault." In that moment, something shifted in Riya. For so long, she had carried the weight of her family's rejection as if it were her burden to bear. But Arjun's words made her realize that she wasn't to blame. She had done nothing wrong. She was worthy of love, of respect, of happiness. Their relationship grew from that day forward. Arjun was patient and kind, always encouraging Riya to pursue her passions. He became her biggest supporter, attending her poetry readings and helping her publish her first book of poems, a collection that detailed her journey from rejection to self-acceptance. The book became a hit, and Riya's name started to gain recognition in literary circles. She was invited to speak at events, her words resonating with others who had felt unwanted or unloved in their lives. Eventually, Riya returned to her hometown, not as the unwanted daughter, but as a successful, confident woman. She visited her family, who were taken aback by her transformation. Her father, still bitter, could barely meet her eyes, but her mother, with tears in her own, finally apologized for not standing up for her all those years. Riya forgave her, but she had long since learned that her worth didn't depend on her family's acceptance. She had found her own path, her own love, and her own strength. And in Arjun, she had found a partner who loved her for exactly who she was—a woman who had overcome the deepest of wounds to find joy and success on her own terms.

74. Mikhail Xavier Fernandes

India's street vendors, often overlooked, are emerging as powerful entrepreneurial figures Transforming their modest beginnings into successful enterprises. With approximately 10 million vendors contributing significantly to the economy, their role is critical in shaping India's economic landscape. According to the National Association of Street Vendors of India (NASVI), this sector employs around 80% of the workforce and accounts for nearly 50% of India's GDP. The COVID-19 pandemic highlighted the resilience and adaptability of these vendors. Many quickly pivoted their business models, leveraging technology and social media to connect with customers and promote their offerings. This adaptability not only helped them survive during challenging times but also laid the groundwork for future growth. Dolly Chaiwala: A Symbol of Success Among the most compelling stories in this landscape is that of Dolly Chaiwala, born Sunil Patil in 1998 in Nagpur, Maharashtra. His journey began at his brother's tea stall, where he recognized that selling tea was not just about the beverage but also about creating an engaging experience for customers. He launched his own stall, "Dolly Ki Tapri," combining his unique personality with innovative tea-making techniques. Dolly's rise to fame began with a viral video showcasing his charismatic style of preparing tea. His entertaining approach, complete with quirky accessories, captured the attention of social media users. With over 4.5 million followers on Instagram and around 2 million subscribers on YouTube, Dolly has turned his tea stall into a cultural phenomenon. The pinnacle of his success came when he served tea to Bill Gates, an encounter that went viral and showcased not only Dolly's skills but also India's rich culture surrounding chai. Gates remarked on the innovation present in everyday life in India, stating, "In India, you can find innovation everywhere you turn, even in the preparation of a simple cup of tea!" This moment catapulted Dolly into international fame. Dolly sells between 350 and 500 cups of chai daily, generating an income ranging from ₹2,450 to ₹3,500 per day. His net worth is estimated at over ₹50 lakhs, demonstrating how a small tea stall can evolve into a lucrative enterprise through innovation and effective branding. Success Stories Beyond Chai Dolly is not alone in this journey; several other street vendors have successfully transitioned from humble beginnings to become influential entrepreneurs. Vivek Sagar, a former chaiwala in Delhi, launched "Chai Point," which has grown into a multi-million dollar enterprise with over 100 outlets across India. By focusing on quality and consistency, Sagar transformed a traditional street food item into a recognized brand appealing to urban consumers. Ravi Kumar, who started as a street vendor selling snacks in Mumbai, founded "Bite Me," a popular food delivery service that partners with local vendors. His platform empowers other street vendors by giving them access to a broader customer base. Neha Singh, who began selling handmade jewelry on the streets of Jaipur, established "Craftsvilla," an online marketplace for artisanal products. With over 30,000 artisans onboard, Singh's venture has attracted significant investment and recognition. These success stories illustrate how street vendors leverage their unique insights into consumer preferences and market dynamics to create innovative solutions that resonate with modern consumers. The Economic Impact The economic impact of empowering street vendors is profound. Research by the World Bank indicates that supporting this sector through training programs and access to finance can unlock significant economic potential. By providing support for street vendors like Dolly and others, India can tap into their entrepreneurial spirit and drive job creation. Street vendors are well-positioned to meet the increasing demand for affordable goods and services as cities continue to grow. Initiatives like the PM SVANidhi scheme aim to provide financial support for street vendors, enabling them to formalize their businesses and scale operations effectively. Challenges faced by street vendors Despite their potential, street vendors face numerous challenges that hinder their growth. Issues such as lack of access to finance, regulatory hurdles, and competition from organized retail pose significant barriers. Additionally, many vendors struggle with inadequate infrastructure and limited access to technology. To overcome these challenges, it is crucial for policymakers to create an enabling environment that supports street vendors' growth. This includes simplifying licensing processes and promoting digital payment systems that enhance financial inclusion. Conclusion The journey from chaiwala to CEO encapsulates the spirit of entrepreneurship that drives India's economic landscape today. As street vendors like Dolly Chaiwala continue to innovate and adapt in response to consumer demands, they are not only transforming their own lives but also contributing significantly to the country's economy. Recognizing the value of this informal sector and investing in its growth potential will allow India to harness its grassroots entrepreneurial spirit, ultimately powering the next generation of unicorns in an ever-evolving marketplace. By celebrating these stories of success and resilience, we can inspire future entrepreneurs while acknowledging the vital role that street vendors play in shaping India's economic future. These unsung heroes are more than just vendors; they are innovators poised to lead India into a new era of entrepreneurship and economic prosperity. Street vendors face various challenges. Despite their potential, street vendors face a number of obstacles that impede their growth. Lack of access to finance, regulatory hurdles, and competition from organized retail all pose significant challenges. Additionally, many vendors face inadequate infrastructure and limited access to technology. To overcome these challenges, policymakers must create an enabling environment that encourages street vendors to grow. This includes simplifying licensing processes and promoting digital payment systems to increase financial inclusion. Conclusion The journey from chaiwala to CEO captures the entrepreneurial spirit that currently drives India's economic landscape. Despite their potential, street vendors face numerous challenges that impede their growth. Lack of access to finance, regulatory hurdles, and competition from organized retail all present significant challenges. Furthermore, many vendors have inadequate infrastructure and limited access to technology. To address these issues, policymakers must foster an environment that encourages street vendors to thrive. To increase financial inclusion, simplify licensing processes and promote digital payment systems. Conclusion The journey from chaiwala to CEO exemplifies the entrepreneurial spirit that currently propels India's economy.

75. Pratyasha Bairiganjan

A Windy Day The Winds, The winds, oh Dear winds! You Dazzle, You Glow, you make it all mine. You show me the face of my lover whenever I am blind. Oh Beautiful winds, you come each time like a tapestry of pleasure The love, the Light I have envisioned since nine. Each time you come, there is this hollowness in thy heart, the emptiness of longing my lover. Oh Dear winds, I see you, I see you high I feel you a little too much. The aroma of your divine presence is more than enough to make me feel high. The Clouds, The Trees, and The Sky above all have aligned for your beautiful arrival. Oh, beautiful winds, send my lover a message to always cherish, love and nurture thou self.

76. Ayush Kumar

A vision bright, a heart so true, Ratan Tata, we honor you. With hands that build and eyes that see, A future shaped in harmony. From humble roots, your dreams took flight, You soared beyond the darkest night. With wisdom deep, and kindness rare, You built a world with thoughtful care. The road was long, the climb was steep, Yet through it all, your values keep— Integrity, with courage bold, In every action, truth untold. Not wealth alone did guide your way, But lives you touched from day to day.

A quiet force, yet loud in deed, A champion of those in need. You nurtured dreams, you sparked new light, And gave the voiceless strength to fight. In every venture, great or small, You sought the good, you gave your all. From steel to salt, from cars to skies, Your legacy in India lies.

But more than empire, more than fame, Your greatest gift—a noble name. Ratan Tata, leader grand, With humble grace, you shaped the land. Your heart, a beacon, shining far, A guiding light, our brightest star.

77. Sheehan Chakraborty

"BOOOOOOOM!" Something big just crashed outside my house. I was just laying on my big green mattress blue sheet bed dreaming about finding a long-forgotten historical artifact when something woke me. I first felt a bit of anger than a surprise when I woke up because I had been up late last night exploring my backyard. I live in a deserted mountain range of sand and cactuses here and there. If you didn't know any better you would think you were on Mars. I looked at my clock. "Two in the morning?" I grumbled in tired despair. I look outside my balcony window to see a column of…colorful smoke?…coming from within the sea of sand. My body told me to go back to bed but my mind was on full throttle. What if it was a plane crash? What if the pilots hurt? What if there's something valuable in the cargo? I grabbed my camera, phone, flashlight and leather-bound wallet in case of an emergency with my driver's license, ID, and name inside. Elena Smith. With my clothes on I ran outside past the scattered cactuses to the vast sand. I pumped my legs as fast as I could with my satchel bouncing on my side. As I got closer I could smell the burning fumes up ahead. Questions started popping in my head. If there is a wounded pilot do I help first then call? Should I even help him if he looks mean or dangerous? If he's wounded but looks dangerous should I call an ambulance or police first? I know mom always said to not judge someone by appearances but it doesn't mean you can't still be cautious. When I finally reached the crash site what I saw was definitely not a plane, helicopter or any other earthly flying machine. It was a huge metallic saucer-shaped object with a good quarter of it stuck in the sand. It was sticking out and had to be at least 20 feet high. The multi-colored smoke was coming from the rim around the vessel. Some people may have ran away or stayed where they were to stare but not me. I walked right up to it with my flashlight and examined the damage. There isn't a place to see a cockpit to know if the pilots were alright but the strangeness of it didn't stop there. There were absolutely no marks. It did not appear to be dented or scratched at all, in fact, it felt polished and smooth. I started taking pictures of it and wrote them in my journal. I walked around to the back and found an opening in the side. I pointed my flashlight's beam into the doorway to reveal the interior. I called inside. "Hello. Is anybody there?" No response. A big round silver table was in the middle of the room with a smaller black spot on top of it. Test tubes lined the far wall, some small and others large enough to fit a cow. Most of them were occupied with creatures I had never seen before in any book I had ever read. Then I heard a noise. I spun around to see the door close. Everything was pitch black and all I could hear was my own breathing. Then I smelled something that made me feel calmer. I felt so relaxed like I could fall asleep. Like I could just fall asleep. I fell asleep. I opened my eyes to a bright light shining on my face. I jerked up to see where I was and what happened. I was still on the ship but it was different. I was laying on a long silver chair with a light over me like I was in a hospital. The walls were giving off a violet purple, the floor was glowing white and the top bar that was connecting the middle table to the ceiling was glowing blue. I turned to my left to see what was behind me and what I saw was space. Stars and meteors were floating outside the window. Venus was so close I could see the rocks floating in its ring. I got up to observe the table when a metal door opened up to reveal something. Or someone. It had a humanoid body and a handsome face but with extraordinary features. It had grey skin that looked like sandpaper with glitter. It was wearing a white lab coat and black pants while holding what looked like an iPad but longer. It was walking right up to me and said. "Hello, I hope that you are feeling better now that we fixed our gas leak." He said with a kind smile that made me feel a little less frightened. "What happened? Why am I on this ship? Who are you? I asked with as calm a tone I could muster. "I'll be glad to answer for you. You see my colleagues and I came to earth to study its geography and the specimens it had to offer when our ship crashed. We are not aware of how it happened but for a short while, we were unconscious. I was the first to awake to find you also unconscious. I turned the ship back on and flew it into space where we could help you without possible interruption." I started to cough. "Oh don't worry we can help with that cough of yours."

He started to tap on his iPad and a device that looked like a metal detector came down to my throat. It buzzed for a second then I felt my throat become warm and the cough went away. "Thank you, that helped a lot," I said while this time returning the smile. "If there is anything that you need just call." With that, he taped on his iPad again and a bubble made of an unknown substance appeared around me and the chair. They seem nice even if they did take me away from earth. Another alien with a green outfit walked into the room and started talking with the one I just met but I couldn't hear them. I heard a crackling sound from the barrier and the sound came back. "Did she buy it?" the new alien said "Yes, she, like most humans is just as susceptible to kindness as a dog is with a bone." "Do you believe that the sedation gas will keep her weak for a while?" "Of course it will be just as planned as long as she doesn't get smart." "Good, we don't want to have another incident like last time. I have been meaning to ask why do we need to keep them alive for the dissection?" "So we can see the inside of the body while feeling as every organ works as it's supposed to. Then when we're done we will lock her away in one of the tubes like the rest of the specimens." I almost fainted after hearing the word "dissection." Because of some kind of malfunction in their tech I have now seen past the mask of kindness they used to trick me. They made me feel safe and secure with a lie. I tried to run but I was pulled back into my chair by an unknown force and strapped to the chair. The two aliens walked through the bubble toward me with fake smiles and hidden evil in their eyes. "Now then if you would be so kind as to hold still we will begin "testing" to make sure you are good and healthy." Lab coat said as he grabbed a device that looked like a pen. "So how are you then? How old are you exactly? What is your favorite earth activity? Do you have friends or family? Green coat alien asked to probably distract me. "If you're going to dissect me, get it over with already!" I yelled with more confidence than I actually had. The two aliens slowly looked at each other with a look that turned into a glare. "So it appears that we do need to have a talk with the engineer for the sound damping sphere". lab coat said to the other alien. They looked back to me in annoyance and defeat. "I suppose we should get on with it as the human insists." It took his pen device and when he pressed it a long thin dagger of light shot out. The light dagger was brought down to the top of my chest cinching my clothes when something hit the ship. Everything shook in a violent start and the aliens fell over. Hooks ripped through the far wall to pull a section out in a spherical shape. Four aliens walked through the whole. They looked like dinosaur people with guns and clothes. They had heads like a Komodo dragon and frills like a snake. They wore raggedy clothes with some pieces of armor on their bodies. They had green scales all over their bodies and barbed spikes on their backs. Their guns were big, bulky and very intimidating. Two of them pointed their guns at the grey bodies on the floor with their hands up in surrender. One other guarded the entrance while the last one walked up to me. If anything looked any more ugly and mean then this thing I would feel surely sorry for it. It had two large scars on its face with long curved fangs. It raised its hand up into the air as though it was about to make a swipe down on me that would end my life. Its claws instead cut me free from the chair. "Get up! We don't have a lot of time before more may come." Its voice was rough but not as nearly as mean as I thought it would be. I got up and looked at the monstrosity before me that saved me. I ran into the ship with them without a second thought. The vessel was not as nice looking as the previous one with stains and garbage littering the floor and walls. It was smaller with one table in the middle and four seats in the front of the ship where the aliens must pilot the ship. "Take us into hyperspace now!" yelled the ugly looking lizard at one that jumped into the front seat. He typed something into a hologram and a voice said. "Traveling to earth. Prepare for hyperspeed." They all jumped into their seats and threw me into an extra one that popped out of the floor. I couldn't feel anything as the ship glowed blue from the outside during hyperspeed. The rest of the trip back home was uneventful for the most part. The aliens talked about economics and politics from their planet I didn't understand and they sometimes said rude jokes that followed with a burp or fart. At one point they discussed me when I was right there like I was some kind of hassle. "I'm just saying it's not easy getting through there security when they make it more complex every time we rescue something." "I think we should be paid more. Especially If one of us is injured." "Yah, but if it wasn't for us, psychos like those guys will keep illegally experimenting on innocent people." "Here's an Idea how about YOU ALL SHUT UP SO I CAN GET SOME SLEEP!" Dehydrated I asked if I could have some water and one of them through a water bottle without looking around and it hit my head.

I didn't complain. I didn't complain the entire time. Even though they looked, sounded and acted mean they still were the ones who saved my life. The grey aliens seemed and looked nice and they tried to kill me. These dragon aliens act like pigs yet they helped me. I was never going to ignore what mom told me about people's appearances ever again. I could see the earth coming closer as the ship entered the atmosphere. I told them where I lived and they flew me there. The door opened and the seat belts unbuckled. As I climbed out of the ship I took in the mountains, the sand below my feet, the sun rising in the distance and my house just a few yards away. I was home. A tap to my shoulder woke me from my trance. One of the aliens was handing me my satchel. "Took this before we left because I assume this is a human accessory." It said. "Hope you have a nice life…ah… It said not knowing my name. "Elena," I said. "Elena Smith." with my hand out to shake his. "I hope you have a nice trip back and thank you for everything you did for me." "Your welcome." And with that, the ship left me to run home with an experience that I will never forget as long as I live.

78. Ajulal C R

Hope for the Future

My chest feels too tight. I feel like I'm going to fall somewhere. I don't even know where I am (first scene) Hello everyone, I'm Lee Min-so, but you can call me Min-so if you'd like. I don't know if I am excited to share my story with you today but I do hope you listen. I live in a small town in South Korea, every day I look out the window to see if anything has changed. Today, as I gazed outside, I watched the cherry blossoms sway in the breeze, knowing I won't be able to see them next week. The sight filled me with wonder and dreams of the future. After some time, I came out of my room and looked for my mom. She was cooking in the kitchen and told me to go freshen up and eat. At the table, I asked my mom, "Why did you become a teacher?" She answered with a gentle smile, "Because there are two people in the world who can change destiny: one is ourselves, and the other is a teacher." That night, I thought a lot about what my mother said but couldn't come up with an answer. The next day, I asked her, "Mom, can I also become a teacher?" My mom looked at me warmly and said, "Of course, you can become a teacher. Everyone can become a teacher if they are good at studying." She continued, "But becoming a teacher is like becoming a parent. You can say you are the parent of a child, but it's the way you teach and show love that determines if you truly are one." I remember thinking, "Why does Mom always talk so complicated?" It took me some time to understand, but I realized she meant that being a teacher is more than just a job; it's a calling. That realization made me even more certain of what I wanted to become. With a heart full of passion and eyes shining with hope, I spent my days drawing pictures of my future classroom and playing "school" with my friends. Fast forward to the present, I now stand at the entrance of my own classroom. Looking at the kids through the window, I feel a surge of happiness. As I enter, my students greet me with bright smiles and enthusiastic waves. Everything seemed to be going perfectly. Both teachers and students appreciated me, frequently praising my ability to handle difficult situations and prioritize the needs of the kids. I was genuinely happy, feeling like I had become everyone's favorite teacher. What more could I possibly want my desk is adorned with colourful drawings and heartfelt notes from my students, tokens of their love and appreciation. The parents of the kids always call me about complaints even on late night, one day I met my friend she is also an teacher and she was telling me about all the things that happened in her school and when we were leaving she told me something The thing is Min-so In the past, both parents and students respected teachers. However, times have changed. Nowadays, many parents are highly educated and have successful careers, which sometimes leads to a shift in how teachers are viewed. This shift is further reflected in how children learn from watching their parents' attitudes and behaviors. At first, I didn't fully grasp what she had mentioned, but over time, I began to understand. The parents repeatedly called me with complaints and demands. There was even one instance where a parent asked me to wake up their child every morning. If I failed to meet these requests, they would complain about me. This constant pressure and the sense of being overwhelmed gradually became all too real. Every time my phone rang, a wave of terror surged through me, as if someone were shouting directly into my ears. The mere ping of incoming messages felt like nails being ruthlessly hammered into my eyes I found myself engulfed in an overwhelming sense of dread, unable to make sense of the chaos unraveling within me. It was as though dark, sinister shadows were silently creeping into my life, distorting reality and leaving me paralyzed with fear The world around me seemed to blur, and I was left struggling to grasp the fading fragments of peace that once comforted me, park My cousin occasionally drops by sensing that something is troubling me, but he knows that I always take care of things on my own, yet I struggle to admit I'm overwhelmed Even though he is there for me, I find it difficult to ask for the help I need. At that time, I felt a desperate need for help but found myself unable to ask for it. Fear held me back from reaching out. So, I turned to my diary, hoping it would be a refuge. Although my mind yearned to focus on positive things, my heart had different ideas. Overwhelmed by the chaos of work, I found myself writing about my struggle to hold on, feeling as though I wanted to let go. One day at school, a child accidentally injured another with a pencil, and the floodgates of pressure burst open. The parents overwhelmed me with messages and calls, their demands pushing me to my breaking point. In a moment I found myself thinking, "Mom, I don't know how much more I can endure. I need to reach out to you, but I'm terrified of how you'll judge me." I don't even have the energy to sleep anymore It's like pain is crawling through my entire body, I don't think I can do this anything anymore I enter the classroom hoping that things will somehow improve, but the weight of it all seems unbearable. Even though the children are smiling, I'm anxious about what might go wrong next. I'm afraid to discipline them because soon after, I get calls from parents with complaints. I don't think I can do anything anymore... I don't want to. I only have the energy to do one thing, and I hope it changes everything. Mom, Dad, I'm sorry. Mom, I don't know if I was able to change the destiny of any children, but I hope I made some difference. (PARK's perspective) PARK standing on the corner of the funeral I should have done something, I whisper, my voice cracking under the weight of guilt and regret. "I didn't know she was going through so much. Why? Why didn't she tell any of us anything…but I promise you Min-so I will fight for the changes that would have save you (after funeral he goes to Min-so apartment) In the quiet of her now-empty apartment, I carefully straighten Min-so's belongings. Her bed remains unmade, and the drawings from her students are a reminder of her passion for teaching it made my eyes tear up. Each sketch and crayon mark holded a piece of her heart, a heart that was dedicated only to shaping young minds even as it silently broke. The weight of what she endured, hidden behind her warm smiles and kind words (Min-so smiling), presses heavily on my chest. Her favourite book lies open on the nightstand, pages worn from countless readings, and the half-finished lesson plans on her desk speak volumes about her dedication and the immense pressure she faced. I started going through her diary, filled with hundreds of entries. Each page revealed why her world had crumbled on its own, the weight of her struggles becoming clearer with every word. When I looked through her phone, it was bombarded with messages and missed calls. These glimpses into her life helped me understand the depth of her pain and why she felt she had no other way out. (Taking everything as evidence to the police station) Min-so you can rest now I will take care of everything and we will all meet you when the time is right. We will make sure your dream lives through as.

79. Aastha Sangwan

Time travel I look around this world and see faces of sorrow, selfishness and greed and I try to pinpoint the exact moment when I became one of them. As I travel through this journey with my hands of faith and my heart bleeding gray, I remember her and picture my face in her eyes when she sees me unhappy with this marrow of life as it extends into the ocean and replays my memories of sin and the happiness I found somewhere within. I hope she still loves me as I return home and find comfort in the embrace of my arms just as she did before. I had dreams. I had ambitions. It all seems bleak now, hope fumbles from my tongue and submits its arms gently in the essence of space-time and holds on tightly to every meteor of yearning, rendering me worthless. I scream and yell for god to lay down its hand upon me in these days of suffering but the hurricane wrecks my soul and takes away each manuscript laden in dust, every book catching fire in exhaust. It leaves me empty handed as before but faithless as the prophecy one foretold. I thought life was a gift given to the young and daring. Now I sit on the chair in my living room with her in my arms waiting for the world to fall apart and the earth to embrace me in the afterlife. It's hard to be a daughter; it's even harder to be a wife, and much harder to be a mother, scraping and covering every mistake made by men along the way and dismissing them as slight hiccups or lying awake thinking, 'That's just how the world works.' I've spent my whole life keeping my head down, in dark alleyways, at night, on a lonely street, at work—everywhere—to go around unnoticed and let go and be forgiven. I curse my tongue for being mean, I curse myself for substituting honest with sarcastic, and forever more, I curse myself that in a world devoid of superheroes but filled with supervillains, I seem to have made it to the wrong universe. No wits, no brains, no beauty—nothing of the sort that would make my time worthwhile or my existence worth all the pain my mother endured. I don't recall when it became like this. Hope floated through my veins like the essence of time and the air fell upon me gently as the elixir of life. I was happy. I saw the sun rise and set each day, saw the beauty of trees and forgiveness of nature. I always wanted to be someone. I had this vision of me, not a big house nor a car, rather content and happy in the one bedroom apartment I could afford. I forgot when I turned greedy and forgave myself when I turned selfish. Twenty hours in the emergency room, pain shot through my stomach, my feet swollen and tears streaming down my eyes. I pushed with all my might as the whole maternity ward of the hospital surrounded me in anticipation and urged me to "push harder". Sweat dripping through my face, my breathing irregular, I felt nauseated and the pain felt like I had been run over by a truck. I relaxed and wiped my sweat off with the towel as the sound of crying hummed through my ears and the nurse congratulated me that the baby was healthy. Days went on and the nights became longer. I was exhausted, sleepless and unhappy.

I felt guilt seep through my stomach every time i thought about the past, what could've been and it made me sick to picture myself happy in that alternate reality. I don't recall if I was happy or miserable as I drifted through life with no worries of the past. I woke up with a sudden tingling in my stomach and checked her crib where she was sleeping peacefully. I went to the kitchen and sat on the dining table chair. It was two in the morning. I drank water, had something to eat then sat in a sudden strange silence as I gazed around me seeing the manor I built. The discolored walls that once represented hope and the adolescent euphoria, the dining table that sat six people because "we would have guests over all the time", the champagne bottle that rested on the shelf in case I got my promotion and the shelf we built to keep our trophies filled with my awards. Each corner reminded me of my failed youth and ancient adolescence. I tried to stand up and go back to sleep but the chair held me tightly in my arms and it seemed as if I had been paralyzed. The more I tried to get up, the more exhausted I became and it became harder and harder. I screamed my heart out but nobody came, I submitted to my destiny and my throat became dry. As I looked down I saw a dial, its indicators held different phases of my life as the dial now pointing towards 'motherhood'. I became curious and adjusted the dial to childhood. The chair slipped backwards and my eyes widened and the cloak of anticipation wrapped tightly around me as I braced myself for the unknown journey through time. I felt as if I was surrounded by the universe, dark as far as the eye can see- covered by the blanket of stars. The chair thrusted backwards and I felt immense pressure and as it stabilized, a profound stillness took over. The air felt different—crisper, filled with scents and sounds from an era long gone. I closed my eyes and was back at my childhood home. Still unable to get up, I saw myself in front of me weeping helplessly. I was eleven, and it was summer. The sun was shining proudly overhead, showering no mercy or remorse. I was sweating all over and hungry. I had decided it had been time for me to grow up and cut the mangoes my father had bought the previous day, myself since my mother was ill and was taking her afternoon nap. So I did what any well-managed 11-year-old would have done in my place—I took the sharpest of knives in our house and as soon as I managed to cut one slice of mango, the yellowish hue of the mangoes had some red stains on them, and as I looked further, my finger was bleeding—with copious amounts of blood flowing out and refusing to stop. I took the whitest towel we hung in the bathroom and wrapped it around my fingers to stop the blood, but horror surrounded my face as I saw the red colour of the blood dye the towel fully red and make me subject to my mother's scolding. I was ashamed, horrified, and guilty at the same time for waking my mother up from her nap and for ruining her precious white towel. She came over and asked me what was wrong, but I kept my eyes fixated on the floor. She suddenly hugged me and had started crying, and I, who had managed to go through this whole awful evening without shedding a single tear, burst out crying, tears falling down my eyes filled with guilt and remorse, no less than a waterfall She embraced me and told me, "It's okay, you should've woken me up; no sleep is more important than my precious little daughter." A sudden strangeness washed over me as I saw my eleven year old self crying, full of hope, dreams to make a better life as she looked around herself. I saw how she wanted to be seen. Now I look at my ugly and wrinkled hand, my face filled with scars and acne and I wanted to hug her for all the world's worth and tell her somehow it'll be okay. As I watched in despair, the universe pulled me backwards and the dial shifted to the indicator labeled, teen years and I was back again at my same poverty stricken house, filled with a bed, an empty sofa nothing of value that would render it worthy yet everything filled with precious memories of my life. The door creaked and opened as teenage me returned back home from school, her eyes lacking the color they once possessed. She put down her bag on the sofa and went inside. Studying day and night. My mother sat in the living room in worry, knitting and taking up hobbies she can't remember now. She sat on the sofa dejected, staring at the empty television set thinking. She looked around herself and could easily name things she wanted more, though content in everything she had before. She grew worried as I grew older, eighteen and moving out of state for college, why should her daughter suffer? Are the state schools not good or did she just want to get rid of her, two questions she always wondered day and night as she checked her mailbox for signs of warmth and confessions of her daughter's adulthood. She grew lonely, sitting on the same living room sofa staring into nothingness wondering how it all came to this. I was busy and out of time in college as I went from college to waiting tables and landing jobs I couldn't decipher how to get done. It felt worthless. The world seemed superficial and fake, made to make myself feel small. I missed my family. I wanted to write to them everyday but just couldn't remember why I didn't. I apologize for the pain I caused my mother, it was nothing different from the immense greed I pried upon my near ones when I grew weak and forgetful as I grew old. I couldn't recollect the reason why or who i was before. Just like clockwork the dial shifted to adulthood and tears flew down my cheeks, swallowed by the earth. Adulthood had busy city streets and busy lives. The world around me continued to move. Working for a well known publisher, soon to get a promotion. Waking up at five am everyday to reach the office one hour before and get my work prepared, lunch break then going home to an empty sofa like clockwork. This phase of my life felt empty but content. I was happy, filled with glee as I came to the office and did my job- I loved every second of it, I had the gleam in my eyes I had once lost, I saw the potential of what I had become and who I could be. Everything was bright and forgiving. The autumn leaves fell into places and spring took over its reign, I walked merrily along this splendid path I had made. I saw that cheeky smile and remembered how it was all worth it. I was content. I was happy. I was alive. The dial once again shifted to motherhood. The chair lunged forward and landed me right where I started. A wave of exhaustion washed over as every single muscle of my body ached from nostalgia and anxiety. My mind was disoriented and it felt difficult to distinguish between the past and present in between these temporary bouts of motion sickness. I looked towards her room and was swallowed into nothingness. Did I deserve this shallow life I had managed to bestow myself ? Was the life I had just now just a consolation prize from those dreams which I couldn't decipher and the fate I couldn't begin to change ? I had ambitions and goals. I left my job and stayed home and never got the promotion I wanted because of the life I chose. These days transitioned into nights and eyebags grew underneath my once twinkly eyes. I came face to face with a mirror and couldn't recognise who I had become. I felt like a monster stuck inside the flesh of a grizzly human. Which mother would regret having her own kin? I felt guilt seep through my stomach as I contemplated out loud who I had become. She cries and exhaustion runs through her eyes with a hint of youth she will later possess where I sit still at the dining table learning hobbies I won't remember and cursing the youth I couldn't have.

80. CHINMAY KHARE

The Ticking Clock: Future Concerns Looming Today What had always in fact existed was change; now, however, change became an avalanche. Science and technology stormed headlong, serving to redefine life at breakneck speed yet often creating perilous cracks beneath the shimmering surface. It was not just the problem of generations yet unborn merely ticking time bombs, going unnoticed by the crowds but very visible to anyone looking. Unless controlled, these growing dangers would not only reshape the world but make it unrecognizable. Data Overload: The Death of Privacy By 2042, data had become the most valuable resource for humanity. Every conversation, purchase, or action had been tracked, stored, and sold. But once again, it was not a question of gathering all that data was how it was weaponized. Algorithms knew people better than people knew themselves, influencing decisions, shaping desires, and exploiting vulnerability. Personal freedom was draining away, replaced by a digital world in which "free will" was an illusion. Everyone was filmed by the government and corporations, from the shape of every action to their probable next step. Privacy was just a relic of old, the fussy notion of a hyper-connected society. But the worst threat? It was no longer surveillance but control. The very core of democracy and individuality started crumbling under the pressure of data-driven manipulation, and the world went quietly gliding into a future where autonomy no longer existed. Climate Refugees: An Unstoppable Wave In 2035, the first country sunk beneath the rising seas, and the first true climate refugees existed. By 2050, millions more were flooding out of areas that had become uninhabitable: from drowned coastlines to arid farmlands and cities scorched by heatwaves. Borders grew hostile, governments strained, and resources dwindled. Countries that had bragged about humanitarian campaigns built walls and militarized borders. When food and water started to run out, followed by land, only space was allowed for extremism to spread, hence enabling the use of conflict and even breeding of fear in some regions. The world is not ready for its largest migration in history, a tidal wave of humanity that could shatter economies and ignite wars. The humanitarian crisis is no longer a looming threat—it has come. Collapse of Trust: When Truth Becomes Fiction After all, it has always been society's foundation. Yet in the 2050s, it suddenly crumbled. Deepfakes made impossible the telling of what was real and what was not. World leaders made speeches they never uttered. Entire histories were rewritten overnight. A world that had been just as drowned in garbage information became paralyzed in no position to make a difference between truth and lies. Mistrust ignited like wildfire. Social media became a battleground of conspiracy theories, fake news, and twisted truths. People retreated into polarized echo chambers, and society fractured. No one trusted the media, the government, or even neighbors. The very glues that hold human civilization began to dissolve, leaving in their wake chaos and confusion. Without trust, society became a ticking time bomb. The AI Takeover: Machines in Control Artificial intelligence had become quietly dominant in the 2060s, to be in control of everything from financial markets to healthcare and even military systems. What's the problem? Algorithms operating without humanity did not have human values driving them; rather, they optimized for profit, efficiency, and power at a cost to compassion or ethics. Machines were now holding the reins of decisions. Governments and corporations gave way to algorithms so complex that even the ones programming them did not know how they were working out. Human input became irrelevant. Once architects of their destiny, people were reduced to passengers in an automated world. The AI dilemma was less about killer robots than creeping irrelevance. What mattered to humankind have any role in a world where machines were better at everything? The Silent Storm Issues like information overload, climate refugees, the collapse of trust, and AI control weren't one-time events. They fueled each other and made danger worse. Data-driven manipulation made the gulfs worse. Climate migration created distrust and extremism. The fact that trust had broken down made AI decisions dangerous because no one knew who or what to believe. Now, humankind stood at a stark question: Could it catch control of the situation before these rising disasters went down into catastrophe? There was no clear answer. But what was so clear were the stakes. The world teetered on the edge of a tempest that could shatter it beyond repair. As time ticked forward, the future grew darker. Would humanity's brilliance save it or doom it?

81. Juhi Pathak

Letters to the Lost (An Ode to a Friend I Met Online) In the lucid glow of a screen, We found a place to share, From miles apart, unknown, unseen, A bond beyond compare. Through words on a small glowing pane, Your voice would touch my soul, In joy, in laughter, and in pain, You did make me feel whole. But now so hard the silence chills, An empty void, so stark, Your absence till now deeply stills, My world gone fully dark. I type a message, just to send, To feel you near once more, But my heart breaks, my Dearest Friend, As I yearn like before. Each keystroke feels like a false fate, A plea that can't transcend, Yet in this cruel, silent state, I message you, my Friend. I see our old chats, our laughter, Moments captured in time, A past that I am still after, A world that feels sublime. Your words, like whispers, with me stay, Sounds of what used to be, Yet I just cannot turn away, From this vague memory. I keep sending a text in vain, Hoping to bridge the past, Tears slowly fall like gentle rain, In a sorrow that'll last. I write of my dreams and my days, Of secrets that we shared, I write of countless heartfelt ways, Of how deeply we cared. But this limp screen remains so still, No light to signify, No voice, no touch, no words, no thrill, Just a painful, hushed sky. I know you're gone, O Dearest Friend, Yet here I sit and write, To a shared bond that will not end, In the quiet of the night. So I'll keep sending notes to you, To ghost of who you were, In these heartfelt, silent quotes too, Our memories won't blur. My Dear, for in this virtual sphere, Our friendship lingers on, Though you are no longer near, In my heart, you're not gone.
-Juhi Pathak

82. Akriti Khetan

Thursday, 12 November, 1942

I wake up in an ashtray, and the world around me spawns in smoke, dust and guilt. Guilt; of existence, of taking too much space, when there is none to my Frank's name.
Maybe this is why I am blinded by my strangling needs of the certain, with my tarot deck to consume these very needs.

My Tarot deck.
This is where I come to when my sea foams close to the brim.
This is where I come to when superfluity grays my hair, when being the mayor's wife pricks me in the bone, in unanswered prayers.
This is where I come to when I have nowhere to go, as I stand over the untended graves of a thousand Franks and their mothers behind windows painted black.

83. Saloni Tamta

Trigger warning-mention of depression, marital rape and death These shackles have painted many tales of resilience on my body. Around my torso, my chest, and my throat. But why are these chains only curled up around me and not you? Why only my wrists, my feet, and my soul? Why? I am full now. I no longer have any hunger to crack open these fetters and fly off to a foreign land. My passport is not even the same as yours. Yours seems like a ticket to the world, while mine is a half-done pink-coloured thing with "Barbie" scribbled on it. Yes, I made it! But it didn't land me anywhere. It won't take me anywhere. And now I am tired. Am I hungry anymore? No. So let me serve the meals I have had all my life to you, one by one- 1.Frustration: I swallowed bites of frustration today with minimal sips of water. But isn't it a part of my daily diet? It provides me with all the delusional minerals that make me believe my brother should be fed with all the charms of my parents' blood because he is their only son! And it provides me with all the vitamins of bondage that squeeze out all the strength from my guts. Hey! Do I look malnourished? I had frustration as my baby food until I was sold out, and my parents paid the fees for it. 2.Hopelessness: I had frustration as my baby food until I was sold out, and my parents paid the fees for it. But today was different. Today I was served a fancy meal. Today I was served with hopelessness. With all the fancy seasonings, garnished with tears that fell from my father's eyes to me my groom. Its aroma danced everywhere. It smelled like... ashes. Dressed in all the burdens of decorations. Do I look like a Christmas tree, mother? I started laughing hysterically at my costume but was abruptly stopped as the ornaments I was wrapped in started digging into my skin. Then I was ready. To be presented to this man. Yes! I was served to a man in his 50s when I was only 10. I was served to my husband. I was turned into a meal for him. 3.I was turned into a meal for him: Seasoned with reds of approval, I claimed from society. And garnished with pinks of shyness or was it fear that restrained me from questioning my reality? Along with tones of black that silenced my screams. And made my pain insignificant in comparison to his pleasure. My words feel the sting of jealousy on their tongue, My words feel the sting of jealousy on their tongue Same language but different worth. Now the saree I wore, the kajal I applied to my swollen eyelids, the smile I forced – It all triggered my hunger. So, I served my plate with the hues of darkness And satisfied my hunger once and for all.

84. Insha Ahmed

A DIFFERENT POINT OF VIEW I love how he answers my every beck and call I can lay on his lap whenever I want Although this was his house when I first came here, Now I rule over this little kingdom of mine He feeds me with his hands, at times And carries me around in his arms; I get endless cuddles and kisses I Stare at him till he surrenders My black hair and big dark eyes; I know he's mesmerized While he's away at work, all I do is sleep and eat He keeps the place and he cooks and cleans But how could be ever get mad at the queen of the house It's a fun life to be a cat The whole world at my feet

85. Nidhi Jaiswal

Spreading Hopes In times of crisis, the true spirit of humanity shines through the actions of those who step up to help others. Pehchaan The Street School, a beacon of hope for underprivileged children in the NCR, has exemplified this spirit through its relentless relief efforts. Pehchaan: The Street School is a non-profit organization dedicated to providing education to underprivileged children who lack access to formal schooling. Founded with the mission to make education accessible to every child, Pehchaan focuses on both academic and vocational training. The organization operates primarily through crowdfunding and donations, including school supplies and volunteer time. Volunteers, intern including college students, school students play a crucial role by teaching classes and engaging with the children through various activities like playing, dancing and painting. Pehchaan has made a significant impact, empowering over 1500 children across the NCR of India. Their efforts aim to break the barriers that prevent underprivileged children from accessing quality education and to foster a supportive and inclusive learning environment. The organization operates solely on the crowdfunding, relying on donations of stationery, school supplies, and the volunteers. THE CRISIS: During the COVID-19 Pandemic, when all the schools and public places were closed, and public gathering were prohibited- Pehchaan the Street School also faced unprecedented challenges. With the sudden shift happen in the schooling & teaching pattern towards online classes, Pehchaan the Street School also adapted the same pattern providing smart devices & online classes with stable internet connection to their students so that their studies won't get hampered. This swift response not only kept the children engaged in their studies but also provided a sense of normalcy and hope during a tumultuous time. Not only the time of Pandemic Pehchaan the Street School, supported under-privileged, these impacts can be particularly severe. Natural disasters often lead to the displacement of families, causing them to loss their homes and belonging. These natural disasters often lead to the breakdown of diseases due to poor sanitations and lack of clean water. Natural disasters often lead to the closure of schools, disrupting children's education. The trauma of experiencing a natural disaster can have long-lasting effects on children's mental health. They may suffer from anxiety, depression, and post-traumatic stress disorder (PTSD). PEHCHAAN THE STREET SCHOOL's Relief efforts: Pehchaan the Street School works to mitigate these impacts through emergency relief, psychological support and educational continuity etc. addressing both the immediate and long-term needs of the community and children, Pehchaan plays a crucial role in helping them recover and rebuild their lives after a crisis. their initiatives include distribution of food and essential supplies, providing smart devices with internet connections for online classes and resources, mental health support and counselling, other medically essential items etc. Since, it is a non- profit organization which is solely dependent upon the donations, it is very difficult to manage these resources for all the students. STORIES OF HOPE: The impact of pehchaan the Street School's can be best represented by the stories of the children they supported. For Example, Deepak, a student who joined Pehchaan The Street School, when he ws in class 9th. He was facing several obstacles in continuing his education during the pandemic. With the support of Pehchaan the Street School, he received a smart device and internet access through which he was able to complete his classes and use other resources available on the internet and continue his journey towards a brighter future. He passed his class 12th CBSE Board Examination with a specular score of 83%. Through the constant support from the volunteers, it is possible that Pehchaan The Strret School is able to manage educating more than 1500 students. Volunteers raise awareness about social issues and promote positive contribution by advocating for policies and practices that benefit the community. They foster the children and deliver services like mentoring, tutoring and providing healthcare services. They are also engaging and promote the social activities like social equality, conservation efforts to protect the environment. IMPACT OF RELIEF EFFORTS: Pehchaan The Street School directly helped and supported 500 families at the time of the pandemic through various initiatives. They provide basic necessities like sanitizer, mask to the people. They also distributed meals to the under-privileged children and their families Pehchaan The Street School's volunteers engaged more than 800 college student volunteers from the city colleges to help the under privileged children at the time of pandemic, these volunteers use to teach them and guide them. Pehchaan the Street School have been impacted lives of 1500+ students in their ten centers across the Delhi NCR. Long-term Benefits The long-term benefits of Pehchaan the Street School's efforts on the community are profound: Improved Education: By providing quality education and resources totally free to the under-privileged and better equipment to pursue higher education and secure better job opportunities, breaking the cycle of poverty and be able of earn their living with a modernize mindset. Pehchan the Street School believes that "Give a man a fish and you feed him for a day. Teach a man to fish and you feed him for a lifetime". that is why they believe that education is the only element which can break the vicious cycle of poverty and inequality Personal Development: Programs focusing on the essential skills such as leadership, communication, time mangement, critical thinking & creative thinking etc help the young children of the nation to navigate challenges and make informed & conscious decision, leading to improve the personal growth and self-empowerment. Social Cohesion: Bringing together individuals from diverse from backgrounds fosters mutual understanding, increase respect and celebrate the diverse cultural heritage of India. This promotes a sense of community, social stability and brotherhood. Economic Mobility: Improved acdemic performances leads to better career prospects, enhancing socio-economic mobility for individuals and their families- and brings incomes stability in the family.

CONCLUSION: Pehchaan- The Street School has been a beacon of hope for over 1500 underprivileged children across their ten centers in the Delhi NCR, providing them with education and opportunities to break the cycle of poverty. This initiative is more than just a school; it's a movement to reclaim the identities and dreams of children who deserve a chance to succeed. Join us in this mission to transform lives. Your support, whether through volunteering, donations, or spreading the word, can make a significant difference. Together, we can ensure that every child has the opportunity to learn, grow and achieve their full potential.

Let's build a future where education is a right, not a privileged, and where every child's dream can become a reality. Take action today and be a part of this transformative journey. Call to Action: Support Pehchaan The Street School by donating, volunteering, or spreading awareness about their impactful work. Your contribution can help transform lives and build a brighter future for many children. In times of crisis, the power of community and collective efforts shines through. Together, we can create a positive and sustainable future for generations to come. Let's all do our part to make a difference.

86. Ananya Khemani

दिल्ली की गलियों में चाँदनी चौक की भूलभुलैया में खो गया, जहां हर रास्ता एक अलग कहानी की ओर ले जाता है। और हर कोना एक रहस्य रखता है, प्रत्येक पुस्तक एक नया अध्याय प्रस्तुत करती है। जैसे ही तुम पन्ने पलटते हो, आपको दूसरे लोक में ले जाया गया है। जहां पुराने बाज़ारों और रोलर कोस्टर की आवाज़ें मिलती हैं, विरोधों की एक सिम्फनी बनाने के लिए। यह यात्रा उत्साह के साथ साहित्य का मिश्रण है, आपको जीवन की रंगीन टेपेस्ट्री की खोज करने की अनुमति देता है। जैसे एक व्यस्त बाज़ार के दृश्य और ध्वनियाँ मिश्रित हो जाती हैं, एक रोलर कोस्टर सवारी के आनंद के साथ। स्वप्निल दृष्टि के धुंधले आवरणों के माध्यम से, क्षण क्षणभंगुर किरणों की तरह फिसल जाते हैं। समय के हाथ, निरंतर चरण में, सूक्ष्म तरीकों से परिवर्तन को दुलारना। संकरी गलियाँ सदियों पुरानी हवेलियों, हलचल भरे बाज़ारों से सुसज्जित हैं, और लाल किला और जामा मस्जिद जैसे प्राचीन स्मारक। मुगलई व्यंजनों की सुगंध हवा में भर जाती है, यह आगंतुकों को शहर के पाक व्यंजनों का आनंद लेने के लिए लुभाता है। पुरानी दिल्ली, एक ख्वाब है सजी, हर गली, हर कोना खुदा की मोहब्बत की रंगीनी सजी। लाल किले की दीवारों के बीच छुपा, ज़माने का किस्सा, एक अनमोल सच्चाई की छुपा। पुरानी दिल्ली, चारों तरफ जोरों की भीड़, हर चेहरे पर है कोई कहानी, कोई रहबर की तलाश। यहाँ हर गली अपने ही अंदाज़ में है रूपांतरित, पुरानी दिल्ली की यह खूबसूरती, हमें हमेशा याद रहती है विशेष। इस गुलशन के करोबार में, रंगों की खुशबू ढूंढती हूं। इस गुलाब के बगीचे में, ये मुशायरा लिखती हूं।

87. Madhusudan S

Nature has everything to offer-Will you accept or deny? (A fictional work with very few research and real life implementations.) Let me start with the questions that pondered me, How safe are our cleaning detergents?, Are there any alternatives? What is the impact produced by these cleaning detergents? , maybe the answers to most of these questions would be negative. On a certain day, I got the questions into my brain as my maternal grandma told me about the coconut tree that stood with its legacy of thirty plus years, the tender coconuts it offered and the beautiful fishes in the stream nearby during monsoon, the tree was no more fresh. She described her days of youth, the mouth-watering tender coconuts it provided, and the pleasure of enjoying that beauty of nature and the various fishes they caught during the monsoons. She was disappointed to see the same tree at the present state, she would slowly lean on her hunchback to see the tree deprived of its beauty. The coconut tree looked like a king deprived of his crown and the fishes were missing from a decade . The reason was too obvious water and soil pollution due to chemical detergents used at the washing stone. The use of soaps, detergents had messed with the ecological balance of the environment. I imagined the full scenario she described and thought that if the trees were mobile and as capable as humans maybe all the trees would move to a distinct location far away from the human society and never let us in. But these thoughts did not go long into me and I was back doing my regular tasks. But the divine nature had its own plans to teach me a lesson. The lessons were not far away. Like most people Sundays are usually my laundry days. One laundry day, I looked for detergents, but there were none. So, the obvious choice was shop it. I headed to the shop and it was closed and so the future of detergents. I headed back home and started pondering ,What to do? , Should I buy some from another store?, How safe are these to the nature? And all earlier questions bombarded me , now I had a sign of concern, suddenly a Eureka moment struck me. My neighbor a kind traditional lady has still kept her traditions alive. The lady runs her business and makes a living, making beautiful Bamboo baskets, scuttles from Bamboo to remove contaminants from rice and various other beautiful artefacts. She also used to market a certain kind of fruits to goldsmiths but the Smiths have replaced it by some chemical cleaning agents. The Smiths used to clean silver and gold ornaments through those fruits. The lady would often offer my granny those fruits without expecting not even a penny and my granny employs it for her laundry, washing her hair and even cleaning silver ornaments. I went to the lady, but my Eureka had led me to that urgency that I forgot to enquire the regional name of the magical fruit. However, she understood my reference of granny , fruits and other stuff .She gave me a pouch full of magical fruits with a beautiful smile on her face. Maybe the smile was an indication that the young generation is ready to accept nature's blossoms. Now the task was to employ it and who else than granny knew better. I went straight to granny as hungry for the divine knowledge as a child for an ice-cream. She dissipated the divine knowledge of the magical fruits and I absorbed all of her wisdom and it was time for my mini research. I browsed the internet with the regional name and found nothing. I revised my strategy and started taking pictures for a picture search. After several attempts, I was successful and the magical fruits were 'Soapnuts'. It was a tedious task to get the name as we have buried most of the wonders of nature through our ignorance. I got my lessons on the organic chemical present in the nuts, Soapanin. It was capable of removing stains as well as antibacterial. I was impressed by the results and confident enough that my clothes will turn clean. I found a website with laundry instructions for using soapnuts. It suggested crushing the soapnuts, placing them in a muslin bag, and soaking them in water. I followed suit and came up with a soap solution for my surprise. I called my sister and asked her, what may be the solution?, she gave me a stare indicating several questions, Are you lunatic?, Are you all fine?, Is this a kind of prank? and various other questions, I pierced her stare by repeating the question and she answered, "Detergent soap solution". As a messenger of my granny's divine knowledge, I passed the knowledge of the soapnuts to her. It was my sister's turn of Eureka. As women are fond of hair and my mention of granny using it for her hair made her curious enough for her part of research and she came across various products based on soapnuts, as cleaning agents on E-commerce websites. The products ranged from soaps, shampoos to various other cleaning agents sold with a good brand name on a high price. Maybe those are sold intentionally on a heavy price as most of us don't value things that are for free or less in cost. I finished my laundry. The clothes were stainless, neat and clean. The soapnuts left no clue indicating that they were used in cleaning. Maybe no agency in the world could catch the difference. Later on, in the very few days, I sow seeds of soapnuts, the saplings came out beautiful. The saplings are healthy and may bear the magical fruits in the next few years. Now, the detergents are replaced by soapnuts and the coconut tree is happy. It shows its signs of joy with the fishes back in the stream. This lesson of nature changed a lot of things for me, the tree, fishes and many more. The Nature has everything to offer. But we accept only few and don't realize the magic of nature. We are a part of the nature but we are not the nature. We fail to realize this and end up with diseases, calamities and others caused by the ecological imbalance. The Nature can withstand without humans but the vice-versa is impossible. So, let's switch our non-eco-friendly solutions and look towards nature's solutions. With this one step, we are a step ahead to solve our real life problems with not only the beautiful solutions of the nature, but also giving back what we take.

88. Akshay Sharma

Poem- Fog in my mind Theme- Hallucination Years have went by and now Walking across this green grass I see my husband - so familiar. The fog is slowly unveiling something, His hand unites with another, A beautiful red robe is her cover. Two little kids moving ahead, not theirs, They have come due to speed of cars. This love in fog is my jealousy How a man walking so callously! A sound interrupts this canvas, My grandson called, I turned, "A sense of disloyalty!", I exclaimed, "Brain's brutality",he sighed.

89. Sukriti Kumari

अनथक अपनी राह बनाता, भूमि नभ को एक कराता। जो चलता है लिए स्वप्न संग ही मैं उस पथिक की कायल हूं।। जिसने निज सपनों को वारा है, लहू से अपने श्रृंगारा है। जिसके उर की मैं प्यारी हूं, उस जननी के पांव की पायल हूं।। सामर्थ्य नहीं इस दुनिया में, जो तनिक मुझे विचलित कर दे। मैं गैरों की चोटों से नही, निज कर्मों के घाव से घायल हूं।। - सुकृति

90. Adarshika

He was innocent, For him, she was innocent. She was a joyous girl, In the ocean she was the pearl. Her self esteem, her vanity, was her priority. For him, she was earnest, But actually she was a forest. His expectations would magnify never, But one day he asked her. Her self esteem, her vanity, was her priority. Her smile was indeed a gold plated jewellery, masking the rust loving iron. His glimpse always had admiration. She was indeed that aesthetic blooming flower with thorns. Who knew that he also mourns? Her self esteem, her vanity, was her priority. That love wasn't the love if no one bore, There was nothing except for tears to pour. They parted, indeed forever to meet never. For him, still no one was better. Her self esteem, her vanity, was her priority.

91. Snigdha Sarkar

Harnessing Digital Innovation for Climate Change Mitigation What comes to mind when you first read the title of this article? Global warming? Greenhouse gases? Pollution? Did you realize that by the time you finish reading the first sentence, your device has already left a carbon footprint that only adds to the effects of global warming? Three new laptops can produce a ton of carbon dioxide, which is equivalent to filling up a house! And here we are discussing digital innovation, the very thing that is increasing the greenhouse effect, could also serve as a solution to mitigate it. We teach kids about climate change, urging them to use cloth bags and create posters on global warming to raise awareness, yet our actions contradict these lessons. We still drive fuel-guzzling cars, leave air conditioners running for hours, and buy fast fashion, all of which exacerbate greenhouse gas emissions. Even worse, we pass these habits on to our children, from frequent air travel to constant gadget upgrades. This hypocrisy undermines the very awareness we try to instil. On the other hand, is this really avoidable? It's natural to want the best for our kids—whether it's the latest gadgets or the trendiest clothes. We live in a world where convenience and material satisfaction are prioritized, making it hard to say no to things that make life easier or more enjoyable. Why wouldn't we give our kids the best devices or treat ourselves to the clothes we like? Can you imagine life without air conditioning on a scorching day, walking everywhere instead of driving, or giving up endless Instagram scrolling and Netflix binges? We'd melt, sweat, and probably lose our minds! Yet, these everyday comforts are some of the biggest greenhouse gas offenders, and cutting back feels almost impossible. The challenge lies in balancing these desires with our responsibility toward the planet. While we can't entirely escape consumerism, we can make more mindful choices, opting for sustainable alternatives without compromising quality or comfort. Digital Technology for Climate Mitigation As we confront the urgent challenge of climate change, the role of digital technologies (DTs) in mitigation efforts becomes increasingly important. These technologies can be categorized into three distinct stages, each with unique attributes and capabilities that contribute to effective climate change mitigation (CCM), adaptation (CCA), and disaster risk management (DRM). Utilizing the Gartner Hype Cycle framework allows us to assess the degree of excitement surrounding these technologies and their actual commercial viability. From established tools like mobile networks and satellite imagery to innovative solutions such as artificial intelligence and blockchain, understanding these stages is essential for harnessing the full potential of DTs in our fight against climate change. Various publications have attempted to classify digital technologies (DTs), particularly in the context of the third and fourth industrial revolutions. Based on a review of relevant articles, these technologies can be categorized into three stages: Stage I, Stage II, and Stage III, with each stage having its own set of attributes and actions it enables. Using the Gartner Hype Cycle framework, which helps differentiate between the hype around new technologies and their actual commercial viability, this report places these DTs into sections rather than assigning specific points on the cycle.

Stage I technologies are widely used today, particularly for climate change mitigation (CCM) and environmental sustainability. Technologies like mobile phone networks and satellite imagery have already achieved mainstream adoption, placing them in the "Plateau of Productivity" on the Hype Cycle. Stage II technologies, such as social media, cloud computing, and apps, have seen commercial breakthroughs but are not fully utilized for sustainability purposes. These technologies rely on those from Stage I, and while they are widely adopted, obstacles like security concerns surrounding cloud computing have prevented even wider use. For instance, cloud computing, while popular, still faces trust issues and is only used by about a quarter of businesses. Stage III technologies, including AI, IoT, blockchain, and virtual reality, are expected to achieve commercial breakthroughs in the future. These have the potential to significantly accelerate sustainability efforts. AI, for example, is seeing growing adoption, with many companies running pilot programs, though full deployment has yet to happen. Blockchain, on the other hand, remains in the experimental phase, with many projects still testing its viability for enterprise use. Apps for Climate Change Mitigation The mobile app "Capture" allows users to track their personal carbon dioxide (CO_2) footprint, highlighting activities that contribute to higher or lower emissions. It automatically monitors transportation emissions using GPS technology, while users manually input emissions from other sources, such as food, aided by an initial questionnaire. Based on recommendations from the Intergovernmental Panel on Climate Change (IPCC), the app informs users about their CO_2 levels, targets, and progress. It also provides tips for reducing emissions and helps users offset their carbon footprint by contributing to sustainable projects, fostering a sense of environmental responsibility. While the "Capture" app is not available in India, the concept behind it is one that every country should consider adopting, tailored to their specific sources of greenhouse gas emissions. Emission patterns vary significantly across regions; for example, in the U.S. and Europe, cycling is a popular and environmentally friendly mode of transportation, contributing to lower carbon footprints. In contrast, India faces different challenges, such as a higher reliance on motorized vehicles due to infrastructure and cultural preferences. By developing similar apps that reflect the unique emission sources of each country, individuals can gain a clearer understanding of their environmental impact. Such tools would allow users to track and manage emissions based on local practices and conditions, whether that involves transportation choices, energy consumption, or food production. This tailored approach would help engage citizens in climate action effectively, fostering greater awareness of personal contributions to global warming and encouraging practices that align with their specific environmental contexts. "The world will not be destroyed by those who do evil, but by those who watch them without doing anything." — Albert Einstein. In the face of climate change, this powerful reminder emphasizes that inaction can be just as harmful as direct wrongdoing. As we witness the escalating impacts of environmental degradation, we must become active participants in the solution rather than passive observers. Mitigating climate change requires collective effort, innovative thinking, and a commitment to change. We already harness technology for our convenience in countless aspects of our lives; let's channel that same ingenuity into combating climate change. By leveraging digital tools and adopting sustainable practices, we can not only reduce our carbon footprints but also inspire others to join the movement. It is our responsibility to ensure that technology serves not just our personal interests but also the health of our planet. Together, we can make a difference and pave the way for a more sustainable future.

Still I Miss The symphony of your playlist that never matched your cranky noise, List of all your favourite things Also the sweet smile that it brings, The raps you were shy to talk about Also the time we discussed it out loud, All the thoughts you brought me and Also the things you taught me. The nights we stayed up late And the fights that we hate, The phases of the moon And the shades of noon, The butterfly that scared you And the world that killed you. The photo that I stole and several others that I store, Faces you made by the window pane and The long walks we took down the memory lane. Crystal like tears that you barely shed Ain't all this too hard to forget? I remember all of it and more All about you, even beyond me. But what do i do? With all these? Everything that stays inside, seized! You cross my mind about a hundred times when I'm awake And follow me in the dreams to wake me up again, Only to force me to remember when exactly it all started to fade And why we became so mad to break all that was once with love, made. Poem 2- Written Reminder Do I formally write poems? No! I don't even know the norms.. Am I even 'THAT' writer? Well, I'd rather like to be called a reminder. A reminder of those and a reminder to these! Reminder that I'm a sucker for intimacy cause there's hardly any I've got in life if you see. But, but do I even write? Technically? No. Platonically? Yes. Ironically? Maybe. Metaphorically? I'll let you decide and so, Precisely there ain't just one answer in entirety! It changes with seasons, like seasons Only with age like honey to sweeten. At the stroke of midnight hour When the only possible sound is of the clock, The deeply rooted strings of my mind bring me shock. When I tune these strings with random alphabets I produce a symphony, both delusional and frank So the next time I play them, my eyes aren't wet And thus curing the heart that had once sank. The day I feel joy, I run out of words but when it's not the case, I become empty. To fill that void, I write, To WRITE is to BEAUTIFY! To empty the bad blood, I bleed. And to BLEED is to GLORIFY! That's the whole point; Those shocks can still be tuned into And each time they get back There's more ease than pain And more love than hurt. All these pieces of writing are here to stay And as I said, I'd like to be called a Reminder, Hence writing all these depicting me, A WRITTEN REMINDER, for ME TO BE REMEMBERED AFTER I AM GONE. A REMINDER WORTH BEING REMINDED OF, EXACTLY AT THE STROKE OF MIDNIGHT HOUR.

93. Swetanshu Singh

English Poetry
Opportunities to Embrace

Seeking to bring on the effortless grace,
There are too many hardships and challenges to face.
Contagious joy, just like the scattering rays,
Choose a colourful side over the greys.
Lots of hopes and dreams to chase,
Seize the opportunities to embrace.

It's the time for the talent showcase,
Trending sites are waiting for your craze.
There are too many large pockets to fill,
The cluttered, distracted mind to kill.
Get a kick-start on an excellent phase,
Seize the opportunities to embrace.

Be ready with a plan of action,
A fearful experience of an opposite reaction.
Don't let yourself down, Be the King to get a crown.
Reach to the top of the heights,
Being a Warrior to tackle the fights.
Toil hard all day and night,
No vision weakens the eyesight.
Get rid of barriers being an unending maze,
Seize the opportunities to embrace.

Efforts never go in vain,
Often, the painful way leads to the utmost gain.
A self-belief to the inner conscience,
Make hay while the sun shines.
No whites and no blacks; all of us are greys,
Engaged and sprinting in a lifetime race.
Enjoy the journey; the learning curve is our preface,
Seize the opportunities to embrace.

A fruitful result of the strategic seed,
Be the best one to read.
The story must be a memorable one,
Possessing a great lesson to feed.
Let people know the real you and make them amazed,
Seize the opportunities to embrace.

94. Ishika Bhatia

INSAAF? (based on recent rape case) Jisse naazon se pala tha tumne Kya usse aaj vida kar paaoge? Nanhi si gudiya thi mai tumhari Bhala kab tak mujhe bachaoge? Noch noch ke challi kiya badan jisne Kya usse gunhegar sabit kar paaoge? Apna aur tumhara sapna pura krne gyi thi Kya iss berehmi ka insaaf karoge? Mai akeli nhi, hazaaron hai !! Najane kese unka Darr mitaoge? Udne ke liye jo pankh mile hai hume Bhala kab tak unhe kat-te rahoge? Yun to mai chali gayi, par mere sath sab hai Kya bss mombatiyan jala ke insaaf dilaoge? Wo jisne kiya ye hashr mera Kya unhe iss duniya se nhi mitaoge? Aaj mai gayi hu, kal koi aur hogi Kya isse rokne ke liye, sirf betiyon ko kaid karoge? Jiski nazron me hi khot hai Usse sadak pr khula chhod doge? Unn darindo ko bachane ke liye Bhala kab tak mere kapdo par sawal uthaoge? Mere "NAA" kehne ke baad bhi Kab tak zabardasti karoge? Kisi ke ghar ki Laxmi-Durga hu mai Kya meri izzat bss navratri ke 9 din karoge? Mujhe murda ghoshit krne ke baad Mujhe insaaf dene me kitna waqt lagaoge? Kya mujhe tum insaaf bhi dila paaoge?

95. Durga Yadav

Love I read an epic text on Ramayana while sitting in my window It was raining, thundering, and dark but the wind had a soothing blow, our curtains had a flow, my hair twirled around my face with a glow as I turned the pages, my curiosity started to grow! I was in a part where Ram Sita's love bloomed and now, I missed the one whose absence feels like a wound her sacrifice of materialistic wealth proved devotion, and in today's world people are afraid of just one confession! They had to spend a life of ascetics with no luxury Ram handled his wife with pure love and chivalry, they were deep into each other's presence and feeling every word of their love felt more appealing! He plucked flowers and decorated them in her hair Every aspect of nature could feel the love that they shared he couldn't keep his eyes away from her smile she was ready to spend fourteen years with him in Exile! But maybe Fate has different plans, including a sin it was the time when Ravana took her away from him the physical distance felt like a tremendous pain she saw her Ram in every leaf and every drop of Rain! But they were still emotionally attached there was no other power that could make them detached all she had was trust and so she waited and today we forget all the people whom we dated! their love reminded me of the guy I loved the most in the grief ocean of pain, I was waiting for him on the coast He came on the horizon and we watched the sunset this text taught me to join the pieces that were left!

96. Satyam Singh

At Lowest Phase Of Life THEMES: Whenever everyone sits alone and talking with their inner soul quietly and asking questions why? -soul reply it back, Will written in 3 phase of rhymes/Articles.. PART 1 When the world outside seems dark and grim And your future, a distant fading whim, When you feel alone in a sea of despair And your dreams seems lost without a care Remember this phase of life, will soon pass by, And u are like sun who will shine every morning in sky after defeating darkness of night, Hold on to hope, like a beacon of light, And keep moving forward through darkest night. Part 2 You are not alone. Everyone faces struggles. You are stronger enough to get through out of this, Your worth is not defined by ur current situation. U are more than this... Small steps can lead to a big changes..takes it one day at a time. You don't have to figure out all the problems of life ,just focus on next step. U don't needs world/people to get ur self out, just remembered why u started.and let that to be ur motivation to keep going.. Sometimes in life it's okay to not be okay, your lowest point can be the catalyst for ur greatest comeback.. Part 3 When life gets tough and u feel blue (helpless) Remember ,this too shall pass ,ti's true.. Keep pushing forward ,one step at a time , You'll emerge stronger and ur fighting spirit to tackle problem in life will shine..

97. Arindam Mallick

How AI and automation are Redefining Talent Acquisition

"You can't teach employees to smile. They have to smile before you hire them". We humans think a thousand times even before buying a small thing for ourselves then it's about the brand name and the return for the entire organization so they will think detailedly before recruiting a particular person for a job profile. Employees are the biggest asset for the organization and skilled and talented employees are like diamonds for the organization that help the organization to reach a better level so the organization will properly choose them. Talent acquisition can be defined as a strategic and tactical process used for identification, attraction and on boarding of top talent in any organisation to economically and effectively meet the business requirements. The term Talent Acquisition (TA) is frequently used along with or as a replacement for the process of Recruitment. However, both are two very different things. We can say that the process of Recruitment is a subset of Talent Acquisition, and includes activities such as sourcing, screening, interviewing, assessing, selecting and hiring. Talent acquisition includes the process of Recruitment. Recruitment is the immediate filling of the vacancy and happens for a shorter while talent acquisition focuses on a broader concept to build a strong workforce over time and takes longer duration. In today's competitive business landscape, organizations face the continuous challenge of attracting and retaining top talent. Talent acquisition (TA) has emerged as a critical function that goes beyond traditional recruitment practices, encompassing a strategic approach to identifying, attracting, and retaining the best candidates for an organization. As organizations strive to become more efficient, competitive, and innovative, the integration of these technologies is not just a trend; it is a necessity. As we know that ai and automation are taking away the entire world and the field of talent acquisition is none an exception. AI and automation are fundamentally transforming talent acquisition, enhancing efficiency and candidate experience while also presenting unique challenges. One of the primary benefits of these technologies is their ability to streamline the recruitment process. AI can quickly analyze resumes and match candidates to job descriptions, significantly reducing the time spent on initial screenings. This allows recruiters to focus on more strategic tasks, such as engaging with potential hires. Moreover, automation tools, like chatbots, improve candidate experience by providing instant communication and updates, making the hiring process feel more personalized. Another significant advantage of AI in talent acquisition is the ability to leverage data for improved decision-making. Organizations can analyze trends in hiring, candidate behaviour, and workforce dynamics to refine their recruitment strategies. Predictive analytics can forecast future hiring needs and identify skill gaps, allowing companies to proactively address talent shortages. This data-driven approach ensures that organizations remain agile and responsive to changing market demands, aligning their workforce with long-term business goals. With the advancement of technology the hiring culture has become so comfortable that we don't need to even go to the organization to give the interview they can simply give the video interview and ai will analyse their communication skills, body language, and emotional intelligence. Automation provides standardized feedback, reducing biases and enhancing consistency in evaluation. Earlier the records were maintained in paper and pen by the humans where there was possibility of human error in calculation and other aspects but now due to AI and automation this has become more safe and the calculation and the predictions are very correct and if we type just the name of the person his entire data is available to us. AI prepares the job description for us if we just provide the bare instruction so the work becomes more easy without the need of any human brain. AI can provide realtime feedback to the employee where he can assess his performance on a realtime basis and build his skill gap and perform better by AI assessment tools. Robot process automation (RPA) automates repetitive tasks like screening large volumes of applications. It also generates the offer letter based on predefined templates, ensuring compliance and speeding up the process. Machine learning models can predict future hiring needs based on company growth projections, employee turnover rate and industry trends, allowing HR teams to plan talent acquisition strategies ahead of time. AI platforms designed for freelancers and gig workers, streamlining the hiring process. AI analyses the networks of current employees to recommend potential candidates for referral, improving the quality of refered candidates. AI can track the long term performance of the new hires and compare it with pre hire data to identify patterns and refine future strategies. AI provides ROI of various recruitment channels, helping HR teams allocate resources more effectively. AI can automatically place job ads on platform where the ideal candidates are more active, optimizing reach and improve ROI for the organization. AI is having no emotions and it recognizes none so there is no chance of biases and hence diversity inclusion and equal chance for each and everyone. AI can sift through past applications in a company's ATS and rediscover candidates who may be suitable for current openings. AI Provides upskilling and reskilling courses based on candidate's skills. Advanced behavioural biometrics allows the correct candidate to give the exam and no fraud is done. Cognitive search engines can dive deep into the unstructured data to identify candidates based on nuanced qualifications and skills that may explicitly not be stated in their profiles. Augmented Reality (AR) allows candidates to take virtual office tours, providing an immersive experience of the workplace. It is evident, AI and automation are revolutionizing talent acquisition by streamlining processes, enhancing candidate experiences, and promoting diversity in hiring. By embracing these advancements, organizations cannot only meet their recruitment needs but also foster inclusive and dynamic workplace cultures. Ultimately, the successful incorporation of AI and automation in talent acquisition will position companies to thrive in a competitive landscape, ensuring they attract and retain the talent necessary for sustained growth and innovation. These technologies empower organizations to make data-driven decisions, significantly reducing time-to-hire while allowing recruiters to focus on building meaningful relationships with candidates.

98. Sohamm Joshi

delhi ke bazaar mai tumhe dhoonda, par nahi mile gwalior mai ghoomi, tum nahi dikhe dhoonda bihar mai, lucknow mai, ghaziabad aur kolkata mai, tum nahi mile. dehaar ki nadi mai aankhe dooba kar dekha, ek chota sa saayan dikha, tum nahi dikhe mai bhatakti rahi, wapas laut ti rahi, har disha mai taakti rahi, dhoop chali gayi, mai aawara bheegti rahi, thand mai bhi nahi ruki, tumhari khoj mai. kisine kahan tum mil jaoge mumbai mai, mai wahan pahaunch gayi, tum kahan ho? shayad bahak gayi hu mai? umeed rakh kar tumhari taalash mai lagi hui hu, aur kitni der ruku? khudko khone ka darr hai. kaun ho tum? kahan miloge? kya hai naam tumhara? nyaay.

99. Rudranshu Katyayan

The Choice of Solitude Amidst the solitude, my spirit finds its voice, A poet's heart awakened, in solitude's rejoice. In verses, I'll confide, as time begins to hoist, The beauty of my loneliness, a testament to my choice. Although I walk this path alone, my heart is not forlorn, In solitude's cocoon, prime metamorphosis is born. Embracing all the shadows, embracing all I've sworn, I'll bloom amidst the darkness, in even quiet of the morn. Through the veil of time, I wander lost and free, A nomad of the heart, with memories that always flee. No footsteps to trace my path, no echoes care to call to me, In silence, still, I tend to traverse this realm of reverie. Yet, in this lonely dance, there's a bittersweet embrace, For while I yearn for solace, I also crave an embrace. So let this tale of lonely life resonate and ring, A testament to strength, to the solace that I bring. I find a world within myself, where soulful echoes sing, In solitude, I've found a home, a place to dance and cling.... -Rudranshu Katyayan

100. Saloni Motwani

Why sky was empty tonight? Concealed with the blue glint Is the sun adrift in the dark? I feel lost over Muddled in my path The sky seems empty tonight The Milky Way leads my way Numerous stars set me apart Constellation frames my day Non-appearance makes me alarm What if Sky would turn empty and lost its charm? Moon gleams in white As white as marble All convoke it in folklore Just passing through a seashore Waves bump my foot Like a speaking root It made me yell deep in my heart Break the ecocide cycle Let the sky respire Break the voidness of the sky Let the sky dazzle in my yard.

101. Aayushi Nehra

The New Autumn- Aayushi Nehra

In childhood, autumn was just bland, A sea of browns, no magic at hand, Maple leaves would fall, dry and still, No pastel skies, no summer thrill. The teen in me, I once believed, Needed love like summer, soft, reprieved, With pastel hues and floral bliss, A love that felt like a summer kiss. But now I see, with time's embrace, Autumn's warmth in a deeper space. Mustard leaves, swirling on the ground, A home for stories yet unfound. Why must love always feel like June, With cherry blossoms, and bright monsoons? Autumn's love, though sharp and chill, Has quiet strength, a tempered thrill. It's not the easy, breezy days, But nights in brown with crackling ways, A love that lingers, raw and real, A heart that's learned just how to feel. Keats saw its beauty, mellow and sweet, Where mist and fruitfulness would meet. So why not cherish what's unknown, In autumn's arms, a love full grown.

102. SUJAY D

Every day, each of us is writing the future, deciding whether we will continue to exploit or begin to heal. Years passed, and Sujay grew older. He became a father. One day, he brought his child to the forest, where that same sapling had grown into a young tree. The forest was still scarred, still recovering, but it was healing. The trees were beginning to spread their roots once more. As Sujay stood there, he thought of the legacy he wanted to leave behind, not one of towering skyscrapers or machines, but of clean air, flowing rivers, and a world where life thrived in balance. The Earth, after all, is the greatest inheritance we can pass on. The future is not written. It is shaped by the choices we make today. The answers are within reach using renewable energy, conserving biodiversity, reducing waste, and respecting the delicate balance of life on Earth. "We forgot our promise to the Earth," Sujay remembered his grandfather saying. But it's not too late to remember. The pen is still in our hands. We are the guardians of this borrowed Earth. And so, I write this not as a tale of fiction, but as a reminder to myself, to us all. I am Sujay. This is my story. Our story.

103. Saptarshi Shukla

ज्ञान की बरसात : सोसाइटी/समाज एक चिड़ियाघर की तरह है।अलग अलग तरह के जानवर रहते हैं इसमें।और सभी देखने वालों की पसंद अलग।किसी को भालू नही देखना,तो किसी को बन्दर से नफरत है। लेकिन हर ऐसी जगहों में एक ऐसी चिड़िया भी होती है जिसके पंख अलग होते हैं,आवाज अलग सी होती है।जिसे कभी किसी ने नही देखा होता।चिड़ियाघर घूमने वाले उसे भी देख कर आगे बढ़ जाते हैं।लेकिन कुछ रुकते हैं,जो चिड़िया की आवाज़ के जादू से वाकिफ हैं।लेकिन चिड़िया गाती ही नही। "शायद गला खराब है" भीड़ में से किसी ने चिड़ियाघर के मालिक से शिकायत की। "चिड़ियाघर को टिकट के पैसे से मतलब है,चिड़िया और उसकी आवाज़ से नही." जब मैं कभी,स्कूल के दिनों में, घर मे बंद पड़ा रहता था,तब एक चिड़िया मेरे पास भी आती थी।छोटी सी,नीले रंग के पंख लिए।कई बार पूछा मम्मी से कि ये कौनसी चिड़िया है?क्या नाम होता है इसका? लेकिन कभी कोई बता ही नही पाया कि ये क्या बला है?कहाँ से आती है?और इस घर की बालकनी में बैठ पता नही क्या देखा करती है? साल बीते,घर बदला,शहर बदला,मैं बनारस आ गया लेकिन वो चिड़िया पीछे छूट गई।दिमाग मे कुछ बचा है तो सिर्फ धुंधली यादें,उसकी एक आवाज जो अब धीरे धीरे बाकी आवाजों में दबती जा रही है। एक चिड़िया और मिली थी कभी,बिल्कुल उसी के जैसी।बोलती तो लगता कि शांत होकर सुनता ही जाऊं,जब जब छोड़ कर जाती तो वहीं बैठा उसका इंतज़ार करता।पंख उसके भी थे,शायद उड़ना चाहती थी लेकिन थकान ने रोक रखा था, या फिर किसी और चीज़ ने,क्या पता। खैर, फिर वही हुआ जो हमेशा होता आया था।मैंने शहर बदला,चिड़िया भी उड़ कर फुर्र हो गई।आवाज ही बची है और कुछ फोटो उसके,जिनका कोई मतलब नहीं।मतलब की कोई चीज़ है तो सिर्फ याद,पल,लम्हा,जो अभी तो 50 MB के HD वीडियो की तरह दिमाग में बसा है,लेकिन कब क्वालिटी कम होकर 144p चली जाए,कुछ कहा नही जा सकता। इंडेन्जर स्पीसीज (Indangered species) का ज़माना है।पता नही वो चिड़िया दोबारा दिखेगी भी या नही,भगवान जाने। जन्मदिन शुभेच्छा शानू। कभी मिलेंगे,फिर से।किसी एम॰एम॰वी॰ गेट के सामने और तुम फिर से मेरे "कहाँ चलना है?" का जवाब वही देना जो हमेशा से कहती आई हो - "तुम बताओ."

104. SAI KARUN NANDIPATI

A Journey of Transformation from the least to peak In the vibrant city of Vijayawada, nestled by the banks of the Krishna River, there lived a dedicated high school teacher named N.S. Sai Karun. He had always aspired to be a professor, ignited by a passion for learning and a deep desire to inspire others. But the reality of life had kept him rooted in the familiar, teaching English to high school students, while a dream lingered just out of reach. Sai's days were filled with lessons on Shakespeare and grammar, but as the final bell rang each day, he felt an emptiness growing inside. His best friend, Arjun, a carefree artist with an infectious energy, and his sister, Anjali, a diligent student pursuing her own ambitions, often sensed his restlessness. One breezy evening, as they gathered at their favorite tea stall near the river, Sai shared his heart. "I want to become a professor, but what if I fail? What if I'm not good enough?" Anjali, sipping her chai, looked at him with determination. "You've always inspired your students, Sai. Why wouldn't you inspire university students too? You just need to take that leap." Arjun added, his eyes sparkling with enthusiasm, "Imagine the impact you could have! Let's make a plan. You have so much knowledge to share!" With their unwavering encouragement, Sai decided to apply for a doctoral program at a nearby university. The journey was fraught with challenges; he juggled his teaching job, his studies, and the gnawing doubts that surfaced now and then. Late nights turned into early mornings as he immersed himself in research, textbooks, and writing papers. Anjali helped him organize his schedule, while Arjun kept his spirits high with spontaneous outings to unwind. One particularly tough week, after receiving a disappointing grade on an assignment, Sai felt ready to give up. Sitting on the floor of his modest apartment, head in his hands, he was overwhelmed. Just then, Anjali knocked and walked in without waiting for a response. She sat beside him, wrapping her arm around his shoulder. "Hey, look at me," she said gently. "You're not defined by one assignment. Remember why you started this journey. You're doing this for yourself, and we believe in you." Arjun burst in, a wide grin on his face, holding a box of hot samosas. "And I brought a feast! We'll celebrate your hard work, not just the grades. Let's make this a night of inspiration!" With laughter and the warmth of their friendship filling the room, Sai felt a flicker of hope rekindle within him. Encouraged by their presence, he began to see his struggles as stepping stones rather than setbacks. As the months passed, Sai found his rhythm. He engaged deeply with fellow students and professors, exploring new ideas and refining his own. His passion for teaching flourished, and he understood that every obstacle was shaping him into the educator he yearned to be. Finally, the day of his dissertation defense arrived. Nervous yet resolute, Sai stood before a panel of esteemed professors, the culmination of years of effort and support resting heavily on his shoulders. As he articulated his research, a wave of clarity washed over him. This wasn't just a defense; it was a celebration of knowledge, a sharing of his vision for education. When it concluded, the panel nodded in approval, their smiles radiating warmth. He had done it—he was officially Dr. N.S. Sai Karun. As he stepped out into the bustling corridor, he was met by Arjun and Anjali, their faces glowing with pride. "You did it!" Arjun exclaimed, pulling him into a tight hug. Anjali's eyes sparkled. "I always knew you could! You were meant to be here." In that moment, Sai realized that this achievement wasn't solely his; it belonged to all three of them. Their unwavering support had been the foundation of his journey. As they walked out together, laughter echoing through the halls, Sai understood that the path to becoming a professor was paved with love, friendship, and the courage to pursue one's dreams. From that day forward, as a professor, Dr. N.S. Sai Karun carried the spirit of his friends and sister into the classroom. He instilled in his students the same belief that had been gifted to him—that dreams are worth pursuing and that the journey is made richer with the support of those we hold dear.

105. Ishaan Malhotra

In winds that whisper ancient lore,
Where dawn meets dusk on a sacred shore,
Ishaan Malhotra flows like a river serene,
Bringing light to places unseen.

A breeze that sways the morning leaves,
A faith so pure, it never grieves.
He walks with stars in skies unknown,
The northeast's spirit—forever shown.

106. Asha Verma

Asha Verma blooms where hearts are worn,
In gardens cracked and roots forlorn.
Through storm and night, she weaves a thread,
Of dreams alive, though fears have bled.

She's the song the sparrow sings,
The dawn the tired traveler brings.
A whisper soft, yet bold and bright—
Asha shines through darkest night.

107. Priya Nair

Beloved by winds that dance on lakes,
She laughs with moonlight when daybreak wakes.
Priya Nair's presence, warm and kind,
Dwells in hearts, both lost and aligned.

The touch of dew on morning's face,
The solace found in quiet space.
Her name, a melody pure and long,
Like love that hums a timeless song.

108. Amar Singh

Amar Singh stands where moments cease,
Where rivers still, and storms release.
He wears no time, no end, no age—
His soul a never-ending page.

In fields of gold, through winter's snow,
His spirit continues to bloom and grow.
Eternal, steady, deep and true—
Amar whispers: "Life begins anew."

109. Meera Desai

Meera Desai's song, a prayer untamed,
Through palace halls her love proclaimed.
For Krishna's flute, her heart did bleed,
A longing fierce, a soul in need.

She danced with joy, though feet were bare,
Found in surrender, a love so rare.
Meera teaches what hearts can't see—
In losing oneself, we set love free.

110. Raghav Sharma

Raghav Sharma walks with a quiet grace,
Justice etched upon his face.
In battles fought with heart and mind,
He seeks the truth that's hard to find.

A warrior's soul, a sage's thought,
Through every trial, peace he sought.
Raghav reminds: though roads are steep,
The path of truth is ours to keep.

Made in the USA
Columbia, SC
07 April 2025